MONOLINGUAL

THE OXFORD

Picture Dictionary

NORMA SHAPIRO AND JAYME ADELSON-GOLDSTEIN

Oxford University Press

Oxford University Press
198 Madison Avenue, New York, NY 10016 USA
Great Clarendon Street, Oxford OX2 6DP England

Oxford New York

Auckland Cape Town Dar es Salaam Hong Kong Karachi
Kuala Lumpur Madrid Melbourne Mexico City Nairobi
New Delhi Shanghai Taipei Toronto
With offices in
Argentina Austria Brazil Chile Czech Republic France Greece
Guatemala Hungary Italy Japan Poland Portugal Singapore
South Korea Switzerland Thailand Turkey Ukraine Vietnam

OXFORD is a trademark of Oxford University Press.

Library of Congress Cataloging-in-Publication Data

Shapiro, Norma.
      The Oxford picture dictionary: monolingual /
Norma Shapiro and Jayme Adelson-Goldstein
            p.   cm.
      Includes index.
      ISBN-13: 978 0 19 470059 7

      1. Picture dictionaries, English.   2. English,
language—Textbooks for foreign speakers.
      I. Adelson-Goldstein, Jayme.   II. Title.
      PE1629.S52   1998
      423'1—dc21   97-21963
                                          CIP

Editorial Manager: Susan Lanzano
Art Director: Lynn Luchetti
Senior Editor: Eliza Jensen
Senior Designer: Susan P. Brorein
Production Editor: Klaus Jekeli
Art Buyer: Tracy A. Hammond
Pronunciation Editor: Sharon Goldstein
Cover design by Silver Editions

Printing (last digit): 20 19 18 17 16

Printed in China.

Illustrations by: David Aikins, Doug Archer, Craig Attebery,
Garin Baker, Sally Bensusen, Eliot Bergman, Mark Bischel, Dan
Brown / Artworks NY, Roy Douglas Buchman, George Burgos /
Larry Dodge, Rob Burman, Carl Cassler, Mary Chandler, Robert
Crawford, Jim DeLapine, Judy Francis, Graphic Chart and Map
Co., Dale Gustafson, Biruta Akerbergs Hansen, Marcia
Hartsock, C.M.I., David Hildebrand, The Ivy League of Artists,
Inc. / Judy Degraffenreid, The Ivy League of Artists, Inc. / Tom
Powers, The Ivy League of Artists, Inc. / John Rice, Pam Johnson,
Ed Kurtzman, Narda Lebo, Scott A. MacNeill / MACNEILL &
MACINTOSH, Andy Lendway / Deborah Wolfe Ltd., Jeffrey
Mangiat, Suzanne Mogensen, Mohammad Mansoor, Tom
Newsom, Melodye Benson Rosales, Stacey Schuett, Rob
Schuster, James Seward, Larry Taugher, Bill Thomson, Anna
Veltfort, Nina Wallace, Wendy Wassink- Ackison, Michael
Wepplo, Don Wieland
Thanks to Mike Mikos for his preliminary architectural sketches
of several pieces.

References
Boyer, Paul S., Clifford E. Clark, Jr., Joseph F. Kett, Thomas L.
Purvis, Harvard Sitkoff, Nancy Woloch *The Enduring Vision: A
History of the American People*, Lexington, Massachusetts: D.C.
Heath and Co., 1990.

Grun, Bernard, *The Timetables of History: A Horizontal Linkage
of People and Events,* (based on Werner Stein's Kulturfahrplan)
New York: A Touchstone Book, Simon and Schuster, 1946,
1963, 1975, 1979.

Statistical Abstract of the United States: 1996, 116th Edition,
Washington, DC: US Bureau of the Census, 1996.

The World Book Encyclopedia, Chicago: World Book Inc., a
Scott Fetzer Co., 1988 Edition.

Toff, Nancy, Editor-in-Chief, *The People of North America*
(Series), New York: Chelsea House Publishers, Main Line Books,
1988.

Trager, James, *The People's Chronology, A Year-by-Year Record
of Human Events from Prehistory to the Present*, New York:
Henry Holt Reference Book, 1992.

Acknowledgments

The publisher and authors would like to thank the following people for reviewing the manuscript and/or participating in focus groups as the book was being developed:

Ana Maria Aguilera, Lubie Alatriste, Ann Albarelli, Margaret Albers, Sherry Allen, Fiona Armstrong, Ted Auerbach, Steve Austen, Jean Barlow, Sally Bates, Sharon Batson, Myra Baum, Mary Beauparlant, Gretchen Bitterlin, Margrajean Bonilla, Mike Bostwick, Shirley Brod, Lihn Brown, Trish Brys-Overeem, Lynn Bundy, Chris Bunn, Carol Carvel, Leslie Crucil, Jill DeLa Llata, Robert Denheim, Joshua Denk, Kay Devonshire, Thomas Dougherty, Gudrun Draper, Sara Eisen, Lynda Elkins, Ed Ende, Michele Epstein, Beth Fatemi, Andra R. Fawcett, Alice Fiedler, Harriet Fisher, James Fitzgerald, Mary Fitzsimmons, Scott Ford, Barbara Gaines, Elizabeth Garcia Grenados, Maria T. Gerdes, Penny Giacalone, Elliott Glazer, Jill Gluck de la Llata, Javier Gomez, Pura Gonzales, Carole Goodman, Joyce Grabowski, Maggie Grennan, Joanie Griffin, Sally Hansen, Fotini Haritos, Alice Hartley, Fernando Herrera, Ann Hillborn, Mary Hopkins, Lori Howard, Leann Howard, Pamela Howard, Rebecca Hubner, Jan Jarrell, Vicki Johnson, Michele Kagan, Nanette Kafka, Gena Katsaros, Evelyn Kay, Greg Keech, Cliff Ker, Gwen Kerner-Mayer, Marilou Kessler, Patty King, Linda Kiperman, Joyce Klapp, Susan Knutson, Sandy Kobrine, Marinna Kolaitis, Donna Korol, Lorraine Krampe, Karen Kuser, Andrea Lang, Nancy Lebow, Tay Lesley, Gale Lichter, Sandie Linn, Rosario Lorenzano, Louise Louie, Cheryl Lucas, Ronna Magy, Juanita Maltese, Mary Marquardsen, Carmen Marques Rivera, Susan McDowell, Alma McGee, Jerry McLeroy, Kevin McLure, Joan Meier, Patsy Mills, Judy Montague, Vicki Moore, Eneida Morales, Glenn Nadelbach, Elizabeth Neblett, Kathleen Newton, Yvonne Nishio, Afra Nobay, Rosa Elena Ochoa, Jean Owensby, Jim Park, John Perkins, Jane Pers, Laura Peskin, Maria Pick, Percy Pleasant, Selma Porter, Kathy Quinones, Susan Ritter, Martha Robledo, Maureen Rooney, Jean Rose, David Ross, Julietta Ruppert, Lorraine Ruston, Susan Ryan, Frederico Salas, Leslie Salmon, Jim Sandifer, Linda Sasser, Lisa Schreiber, Mary Segovia, Abe Shames, Debra Shaw, Stephanie Shipp, Pat Singh, Mary Sklavos, Donna Stark, Claire Cocoran Stehling, Lynn Sweeden, Joy Tesh, Sue Thompson, Christine Tierney, Laura Topete, Carmen Villanueva, Laura Webber, Renée Weiss, Beth Winningham, Cindy Wislofsky, Judy Wood, Paula Yerman.

A special thanks to Marna Shulberg and the students of the Saticoy Branch of Van Nuys Community Adult School.

We would also like to thank the following individuals and organizations who provided their expertise:

Carl Abato, Alan Goldman, Dr. Larry Falk, Caroll Gray, Henry Haskell, Susan Haskell, Los Angeles Fire Department, Malcolm Loeb, Barbara Lozano, Lorne Dubin, United Farm Workers.

Authors' Acknowledgments

Throughout our careers as English language teachers, we have found inspiration in many places—in the classroom with our remarkable students, at schools, conferences, and workshops with our fellow teachers, and with our colleagues at the ESL Teacher Institute. We are grateful to be part of this international community.

We would like to sincerely thank and acknowledge Eliza Jensen, the project's Senior Editor. Without Eliza, this book would not have been possible. Her indomitable spirit, commitment to clarity, and unwavering advocacy allowed us to realize the book we envisioned.

Creating this dictionary was a collaborative effort and it has been our privilege to work with an exceptionally talented group of individuals who, along with Eliza Jensen, make up the Oxford Picture Dictionary team. We deeply appreciate the contributions of the following people:

Lynn Luchetti, Art Director, whose aesthetic sense and sensibility guided the art direction of this book,

Susan Brorein, Senior Designer, who carefully considered the design of each and every page,

Klaus Jekeli, Production Editor, who pored over both manuscript and art to ensure consistency and accuracy, and

Tracy Hammond, Art Buyer, who skillfully managed thousands of pieces of art and reference material.

We also want to thank Susan Mazer, the talented artist who was by our side for the initial problem-solving and Mary Chandler who also lent her expertise to the project.

We have learned much working with Marjorie Fuchs, Lori Howard, and Renée Weiss, authors of the dictionary's ancillary materials. We thank them for their on-going contributions to the dictionary program.

We must make special mention of Susan Lanzano, Editorial Manager, whose invaluable advice, insights, and queries were an integral part of the writing process.

This book is dedicated to my husband, Neil Reichline, who has encouraged me to take the road less traveled, and to my sons, Eli and Alex, who have allowed me to sit at their baseball games with my yellow notepad. —NS

This book is lovingly dedicated to my husband, Gary and my daughter, Emily Rose, both of whom hugged me tight and let me work into the night. —JAG

A Letter to the Teacher

Welcome to The Oxford Picture Dictionary.

This comprehensive vocabulary resource provides you and your students with over 3,700 words, each defined by engaging art and presented in a meaningful context. *The Oxford Picture Dictionary* enables your students to learn and use English in all aspects of their daily lives. The 140 key topics cover home and family, the workplace, the community, health care, and academic studies. The topics are organized into 12 thematic units that are based on the curriculum of beginning and low-intermediate level English language coursework. The word lists of the dictionary include both single word entries and verb phrases. Many of the prepositions and adjectives are presented in phrases as well, demonstrating the natural use of words in conjunction with one another.

The Oxford Picture Dictionary uses a variety of visual formats, each suited to the topic being represented. Where appropriate, word lists are categorized and pages are divided into sections, allowing you to focus your students' attention on one aspect of a topic at a time.

Within the word lists:

- nouns, adjectives, prepositions, and adverbs are numbered,
- verbs are bolded and identified by letters, and
- targeted prepositions and adjectives within phrases are bolded.

The dictionary includes a variety of exercises and self access tools that will guide your students towards accurate and fluent use of the new words.

- Exercises at the bottom of the pages provide vocabulary development through pattern practice, application of the new language to other topics, and personalization questions.

- An alphabetical index assists students in locating all words and topics in the dictionary.

- A phonetic listing for each word in the index and a pronunciation guide give students the key to accurate pronunciation.

- A verb index of all the verbs presented in the dictionary provides students with information on the present, past, and past participle forms of the verbs.

The Oxford Picture Dictionary is the core of *The Oxford Picture Dictionary Program* which includes a *Dictionary Cassette,* a *Teacher's Book* and its companion *Focused Listening Cassette, Beginning* and *Intermediate Workbooks, Classic Classroom Activities* (a photocopiable activity book), *Overhead Transparencies,* and *Read All About It 1* and *2.* Bilingual editions of *The Oxford Picture Dictionary* are available in Spanish, Chinese, Vietnamese, and many other languages.

TEACHING THE VOCABULARY

Your students' needs and your own teaching philosophy will dictate how you use *The Oxford Picture Dictionary* with your students. The following general guidelines, however, may help you adapt the dictionary's pages to your particular course and students. (For topic-specific, step-by-step guidelines and activities for presenting and practicing the vocabulary on each dictionary page see the *Oxford Picture Dictionary Teacher's Book.*)

Preview the topic

A good way to begin any lesson is to talk with students to determine what they already know about the topic. Some different ways to do this are:

- Ask general questions related to the topic;

- Have students brainstorm a list of words they know from the topic; or

- Ask questions about the picture(s) on the page.

Present the vocabulary

Once you've discovered which words your students already know, you are ready to focus on presenting the words they need. Introducing 10–15 new words in a lesson allows students to really learn the new words. On pages where the word lists are longer, and students are unfamiliar with many of the words, you may wish to introduce the words by categories or sections, or simply choose the words you want in the lesson.

Here are four different presentation techniques. The techniques you choose will depend on the topic being studied and the level of your students.

- Say each new word and describe or define it within the context of the picture.

- Demonstrate verbs or verb sequences for the students, and have volunteers demonstrate the actions as you say them.

- Use Total Physical Response commands to build comprehension of the vocabulary: *Put the pencil on your book. Put it on your notebook. Put it on your desk.*

- Ask a series of questions to build comprehension and give students an opportunity to say the new words:

▶ Begin with *yes/no* questions. *Is #16 chalk?* (yes)

▶ Progress to *or* questions. *Is #16 chalk or a marker?* (chalk)

▶ Finally, ask *Wh* questions.

What can I use to write on this paper? (a marker/ Use a marker.)

Check comprehension

Before moving on to the practice stage, it is helpful to be sure all students understand the target vocabulary. There are many different things you can do to check students' understanding. Here are two activities to try:

• Tell students to open their books and point to the items they hear you say. Call out target vocabulary at random as you walk around the room checking to see if students are pointing to the correct pictures.

• Make true/false statements about the target vocabulary. Have students hold up two fingers for true, three fingers for false. *You can write with a marker.* [two fingers] *You raise your notebook to talk to the teacher.* [three fingers]

Take a moment to review any words with which students are having difficulty before beginning the practice activities.

Practice the vocabulary

Guided practice activities give your students an opportunity to use the new vocabulary in meaningful communication. The exercises at the bottom of the pages are one source of guided practice activities.

• **Talk about...** This activity gives students an opportunity to practice the target vocabulary through sentence substitutions with meaningful topics.

e.g. **Talk about your feelings.**

I feel <u>happy</u> when I see my friends.

• **Practice...** This activity gives students practice using the vocabulary within common conversational functions such as making introductions, ordering food, making requests, etc.

e.g. **Practice asking for things in the dining room.**

Please pass <u>the platter</u>.

May I have <u>the creamer</u>?

Could I have <u>a fork</u>, please?

• **Use the new language.** This activity asks students to brainstorm words within various categories, or may

ask them to apply what they have learned to another topic in the dictionary. For example, on *Colors*, page 12, students are asked to look at *Clothing I*, pages 64–65, and name the colors of the clothing they see.

• **Share your answers.** These questions provide students with an opportunity to expand their use of the target vocabulary in personalized discussion. Students can ask and answer these questions in whole class discussions, pair or group work, or they can write the answers as journal entries.

Further guided and communicative practice can be found in the *Oxford Picture Dictionary Teacher's Book* and in *Classic Classroom Activities*. The *Oxford Picture Dictionary Beginning* and *Intermediate Workbooks* and *Read All About It 1* and *2* provide your students with controlled and communicative reading and writing practice.

We encourage you to adapt the materials to suit the needs of your classes, and we welcome your comments and ideas. Write to us at:

Oxford University Press
ESL Department
198 Madison Avenue
New York, NY 10016

Jayme Adelson-Goldstein

Norma Shapiro

A Letter to the Student

Dear Student of English,

Welcome to *The Oxford Picture Dictionary*. The more than 3,700 words in this book will help you as you study English.

Each page in this dictionary teaches about a specific topic. The topics are grouped together in units. All pages in a unit have the same color and symbol. For example, each page in the Food unit has this symbol:

On each page you will see pictures and words. The pictures have numbers or letters that match the numbers or letters in the word lists. Verbs (action words) are identified by letters and all other words are identified by numbers.

How to find words in this book

- Use the Table of Contents, pages vii–ix.
  Look up the general topic you want to learn about.

- Use the Index, pages 173–205.
  Look up individual words in alphabetical (A–Z) order.

- Go topic by topic.
  Look through the book until you find something that interests you.

How to use the Index

When you look for a word in the index this is what you will see:

the word   the number (or letter) in the word list

apples [ăp/əlz] **50**–4

the pronunciation   the page number

If the word is on one of the maps, pages 122–125, you will find it in the Geographical Index on pages 206–208.

How to use the Verb Guide

When you want to know the past form of a verb or its past participle form, look up the verb in the verb guide. The regular verbs and their spelling changes are listed on pages 170–171. The simple form, past form, and past participle form of irregular verbs are listed on page 172.

Workbooks

There are two workbooks to help you practice the new words:
The Oxford Picture Dictionary Beginning and *Intermediate Workbooks*.

As authors and teachers we both know how difficult English can be (and we're native speakers!). When we wrote this book, we asked teachers and students from the U.S. and other countries for their help and ideas. We hope their ideas and ours will help you. Please write to us with your comments or questions at:

Oxford University Press
ESL Department
198 Madison Avenue
New York, NY 10016

We wish you success!

Jayme Adelson-Goldstein   Norma Shapiro

Contents

1. Everyday Language

2. People

3. Housing

4. Food

Contents

Contents

1. chalkboard
2. screen
3. student
4. overhead projector
5. teacher
6. desk
7. chair/seat

A. Raise your hand.

B. Talk to the teacher.

C. Listen to a cassette.

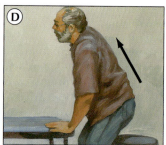

D. Stand up.

E. Sit down./Take a seat.

F. Point to the picture.

G. Write on the board.

H. Erase the board.

I. Open your book.

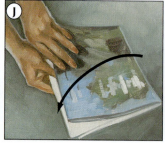

J. Close your book.

K. Take out your pencil.

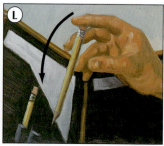

L. Put away your pencil.

8. bookcase	**10.** clock	**12.** map	**14.** bulletin board
9. globe	**11.** cassette player	**13.** pencil sharpener	**15.** computer

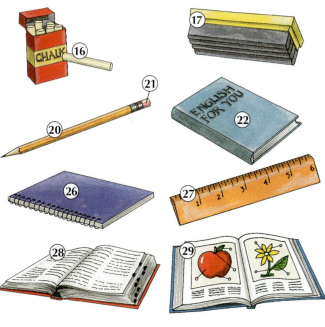

16. chalk	**20.** pencil	**24.** binder/notebook	**28.** dictionary
17. chalkboard eraser	**21.** pencil eraser	**25.** notebook paper	**29.** picture dictionary
18. pen	**22.** textbook	**26.** spiral notebook	**30.** the alphabet
19. marker	**23.** workbook	**27.** ruler	**31.** numbers

Use the new language.

1. Name three things you can open.

2. Name three things you can put away.

3. Name three things you can write with.

Share your answers.

1. Do you like to raise your hand?

2. Do you ever listen to cassettes in class?

3. Do you ever write on the board?

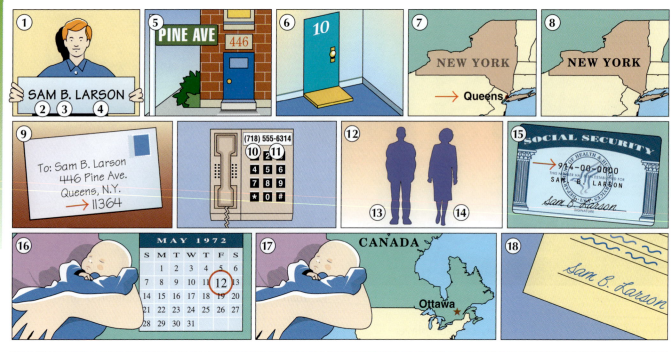

School Registration Form

1. name _____

       2. first name   **3.** middle initial   **4.** last name

5. address _____   **6.** apt. # * _____

7. city _____   **8.** state _____   **9.** ZIP code _____

(   ) _____   _____ _ __ _ _____

10. area code   **11.** telephone number   **12.** sex: **13.** ☐ male   **15.** Social Security number

                                         14. ☐ female

16. date of birth _____   **17.** place of birth _____

          (month)   (date)   (year)

                                  18. signature _____

* apt. # = apartment number

A. Spell your name.

B. Fill out a form.

C. Print your name.

D. Sign your name.

Talk about yourself.

My first name is _Sam_.

My last name is spelled _L-A-R-S-O-N_.

I come from _Ottawa_.

Share your answers.

1. Do you like your first name?

2. Is your last name from your mother? father? husband?

3. What is your middle name?

1. classroom

2. teacher

3. auditorium

4. cafeteria

5. lunch benches

6. library

7. lockers

8. rest rooms

9. gym

10. bleachers

11. track

12. field

13. principal's office

14. principal

15. counselor's office

16. counselor

17. main office

18. clerk

More vocabulary

instructor: teacher

coach: gym teacher

administrator: principal or other school supervisor

Share your answers.

1. Do you ever talk to the principal of your school?

2. Is there a place for you to eat at your school?

3. Does your school look the same as or different from the one in the picture?

Studying

Dictionary work

A. Look up a word.

B. Read the word.

C. Say the word.

D. Repeat the word.

E. Spell the word.

F. Copy the word.

Work with a partner

G. Ask a question.

H. Answer a question.

I. Share a book.

J. Help your partner.

Work in a group

K. Brainstorm a list.

L. Discuss the list.

M. Draw a picture.

N. Dictate a sentence.

Class work

O. Pass out the papers.

P. Talk with each other.

Q. Collect the papers.

Follow directions

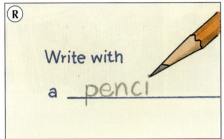

R. Fill in the blank.

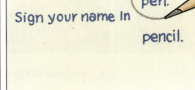

S. Circle the answer.

T. Mark the answer sheet.

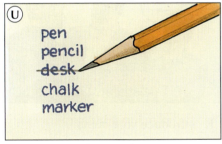

U. Cross out the word.

V. Underline the word.

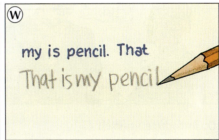

W. Put the words **in order.**

X. Match the items.

Y. Check your work.

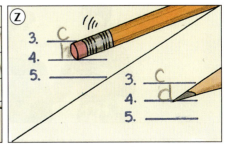

Z. Correct the mistake.

Share your answers.

1. Do you like to work in groups?
2. Do you like to share books?
3. Do you like to answer questions?
4. Is it easy for you to talk with your classmates?
5. Do you always check your work?
6. Do you cross out your mistakes or erase them?

A. greet someone

B. begin a conversation

C. end the conversation

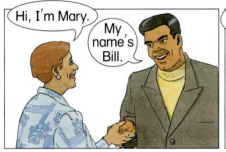

D. introduce yourself

E. make sure you **understand**

F. introduce your friend

G. compliment your friend   **H. thank** your friend

I. apologize

Practice introductions.

Hi, I'm Sam Jones and this is my friend, Pat Green.

  Nice to meet you. I'm Tomas Garcia.

Practice giving compliments.

That's a great sweater, Tomas.

  Thanks Pat. I like your shoes.

Look at **Clothing I,** pages **64–65** for more ideas.

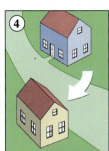

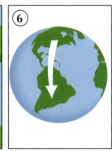

1. telephone / phone
2. receiver
3. cord
4. local call
5. long-distance call
6. international call
7. operator
8. directory assistance (411)
9. emergency service (911)
10. phone card
11. pay phone
12. cordless phone
13. cellular phone
14. answering machine
15. telephone book
16. pager

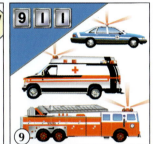

Using a pay phone

A. **Pick up** the receiver.
B. **Listen** for the dial tone.
C. **Deposit** coins.
D. **Dial** the number.
E. **Leave** a message.
F. **Hang up** the receiver.

More vocabulary
When you get a person or place that you didn't want to call, we say you have the **wrong number.**

Share your answers.
1. What kinds of calls do you make?
2. How much does it cost to call your country?
3. Do you like to talk on the telephone?

Weather

Temperature

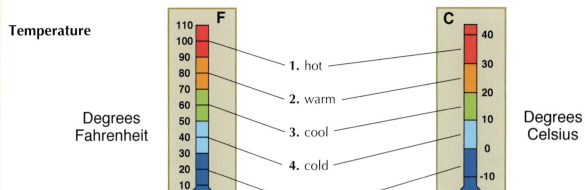

F

110
100
90
80
70
60
50
40
30
20
10

Degrees
Fahrenheit

C

40
30
20
10
0
-10

Degrees
Celsius

1. hot
2. warm
3. cool
4. cold
5. freezing

6. sunny/clear   7. cloudy   8. raining   9. snowing

98° 99° 97° 99°

10. windy   13. icy   16. thunderstorm   19. hail

11. foggy   14. smoggy   17. lightning   20. snowstorm

12. humid   15. heat wave   18. hailstorm   21. dust storm

Language note: *it is, there is*

For **1–14** we use,   *It's <u>cloudy</u>.*

For **15–21** we use,   *There's <u>a heat wave</u>.*
                         There's <u>lightning</u>.

Talk about the weather.

Today it's <u>hot</u>. It's <u>98 degrees</u>.

Yesterday it was <u>warm</u>. It was <u>85 degrees</u>.

1. **little** hand

2. **big** hand

3. **fast** driver

4. **slow** driver

5. **hard** chair

6. **soft** chair

7. **thick** book/ **fat** book

8. **thin** book

9. **full** glass

10. **empty** glass

11. **noisy** children/ **loud** children

12. **quiet** children

13. **heavy** box

14. **light** box

15. **neat** closet

16. **messy** closet

17. **good** dog

18. **bad** dog

19. **expensive** ring

20. **cheap** ring

21. **beautiful** view

22. **ugly** view

23. **easy** problem

24. **difficult** problem/ **hard** problem

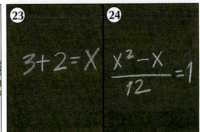
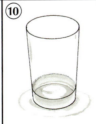

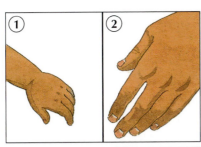

$3+2=X \quad \frac{x^2-x}{12}=1$

Use the new language.

1. Name three things that are thick.

2. Name three things that are soft.

3. Name three things that are heavy.

Share your answers.

1. Are you a slow driver or a fast driver?

2. Do you have a neat closet or a messy closet?

3. Do you like loud or quiet parties?

Colors

1. blue	**6.** orange	**11.** brown
2. dark blue	**7.** purple	**12.** yellow
3. light blue	**8.** green	**13.** red
4. turquoise	**9.** beige	**14.** white
5. gray	**10.** pink	**15.** black

Use the new language.

Look at **Clothing I,** pages **64–65.**

Name the colors of the clothing you see.

That's a dark blue suit.

Share your answers.

1. What colors are you wearing today?
2. What colors do you like?
3. Is there a color you don't like? What is it?

12

1. The red box is **next to** the yellow box, **on the left.**

2. The yellow box is **next to** the red box, **on the right.**

3. The turquoise box is **behind** the gray box.

4. The gray box is **in front of** the turquoise box.

5. The dark blue box is **in** the beige box.

6. The green box is **above** the orange box.

7. The orange box is **below** the green box.

8. The white box is **on** the black box.

9. The black box is **under** the white box.

10. The pink box is **between** the purple box and the brown box.

More vocabulary

near: in the same area
*The white box is **near** the black box.*

far from: not near
*The red box is **far from** the black box.*

HOME	1 8
VISITOR	2 2

SAN DIEGO
235 miles

Cardinals

0 zero	11 eleven	21 twenty-one	101 one hundred one
1 one	12 twelve	22 twenty-two	1,000 one thousand
2 two	13 thirteen	30 thirty	1,001 one thousand one
3 three	14 fourteen	40 forty	10,000 ten thousand
4 four	15 fifteen	50 fifty	100,000 one hundred thousand
5 five	16 sixteen	60 sixty	1,000,000 one million
6 six	17 seventeen	70 seventy	1,000,000,000 one billion
7 seven	18 eighteen	80 eighty	
8 eight	19 nineteen	90 ninety	
9 nine	20 twenty	100 one hundred	
10 ten			

Ordinals

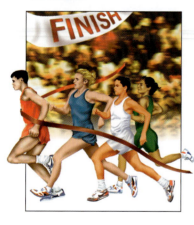

1st first	8th eighth	15th fifteenth
2nd second	9th ninth	16th sixteenth
3rd third	10th tenth	17th seventeenth
4th fourth	11th eleventh	18th eighteenth
5th fifth	12th twelfth	19th nineteenth
6th sixth	13th thirteenth	20th twentieth
7th seventh	14th fourteenth	

Roman numerals

I	= 1	VII	= 7	XXX	= 30
II	= 2	VIII	= 8	XL	= 40
III	= 3	IX	= 9	L	= 50
IV	= 4	X	= 10	C	= 100
V	= 5	XV	= 15	D	= 500
VI	= 6	XX	= 20	M	= 1,000

Fractions

1. 1/8   one-eighth

2. 1/4   one-fourth

3. 1/3   one-third

4. 1/2   one-half

5. 3/4   three-fourths

6. 1   whole

Percents

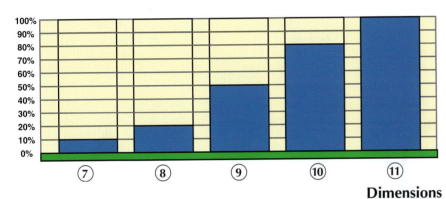

7. 10%   ten percent

8. 20%   twenty percent

9. 50%   fifty percent

10. 80%   eighty percent

11. 100%   one hundred percent

Measurement

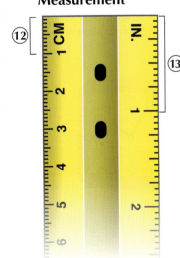

12. centimeter [cm]

13. inch [in.]

Equivalencies

1 inch = 2.54 centimeters
1 yard = .91 meters
1 mile = 1.6 kilometers

12 inches   = 1 foot
3 feet   = 1 yard
1,760 yards = 1 mile

Dimensions

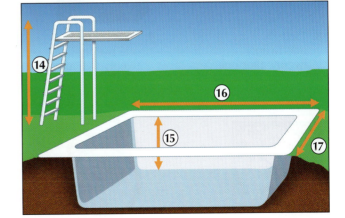

14. height

15. depth

16. length

17. width

More vocabulary

measure: to find the size or amount of something

count: to find the total number of something

Share your answers.

1. How many students are in class today?

2. Who was the first person in class today?

3. How far is it from your home to your school?

1. second

2. minute **3.** hour

A.M.

P.M.

4. 1:00
one o'clock

5. 1:05
one-oh-five
five after one

6. 1:10
one-ten
ten after one

7. 1:15
one-fifteen
a quarter after one

8. 1:20
one-twenty
twenty after one

9. 1:25
one twenty-five
twenty-five after one

10. 1:30
one-thirty
half past one

11. 1:35
one thirty-five
twenty-five to two

12. 1:40
one-forty
twenty to two

13. 1:45
one forty-five
a quarter to two

14. 1:50
one-fifty
ten to two

15. 1:55
one fifty-five
five to two

Talk about the time.

What time is it? It's 10:00 a.m.

What time do you wake up on weekdays? At 6:30 a.m.

What time do you wake up on weekends? At 9:30 a.m.

Share your answers.

1. How many hours a day do you study English?

2. You are meeting friends at 1:00. How long will you wait for them if they are late?

16. morning

17. noon

18. afternoon

19. evening

20. night

21. midnight

22. early

23. late

TIME ZONES

24. Hawaii-Aleutian time

25. Alaska time

26. Pacific time

27. mountain time

28. central time

29. eastern time

30. Atlantic time

31. Newfoundland time

32. standard time

33. daylight saving time

More vocabulary

on time: not early and not late

He's **on time.**

Share your answers.

1. When do you watch television? study? do housework?

2. Do you come to class on time? early? late?

Days of the week

1. Sunday
2. Monday
3. Tuesday
4. Wednesday
5. Thursday
6. Friday
7. Saturday
8. year
9. month
10. day
11. week
12. weekdays
13. weekend
14. date
15. today
16. tomorrow
17. yesterday
18. last week
19. this week
20. next week
21. every day
22. once a week
23. twice a week
24. three times a week

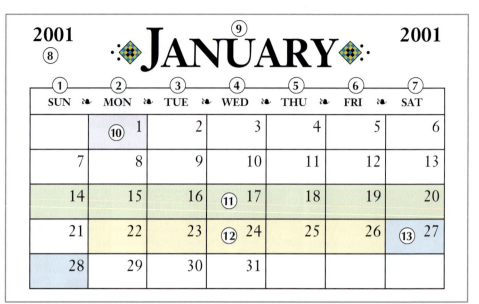

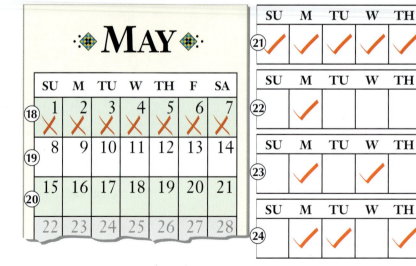

Talk about the calendar.

What's today's date? It's March 10th.

What day is it? It's Tuesday.

What day was yesterday? It was Monday.

Share your answers.

1. How often do you come to school?
2. How long have you been in this school?

2001

JAN (25)
SUN	MON	TUE	WED	THU	FRI	SAT
	1	2	3	4	5	6
7	8	9	10	11	12	13
14	15	16	17	18	19	20
21	22	23	24	25	26	27
28	29	30	31			

FEB (26)
SUN	MON	TUE	WED	THU	FRI	SAT
				1	2	3
4	5	6	7	8	9	10
11	12	13	14	15	16	17
18	19	20	21	22	23	24
25	26	27	28			

MAR (27)
SUN	MON	TUE	WED	THU	FRI	SAT
				1	2	3
4	5	6	7	8	9	10
11	12	13	14	15	16	17
18	19	20	21	22	23	24
25	26	27	28	29	30	31

APR (28)
SUN	MON	TUE	WED	THU	FRI	SAT
1	2	3	4	5	6	7
8	9	10	11	12	13	14
15	16	17	18	19	20	21
22	23	24	25	26	27	28
29	30					

MAY (29)
SUN	MON	TUE	WED	THU	FRI	SAT
		1	2	3	4	5
6	7	8	9	10	11	12
13	14	15	16	17	18	19
20	21	22	23	24	25	26
27	28	29	30	31		

JUN (30)
SUN	MON	TUE	WED	THU	FRI	SAT
					1	2
3	4	5	6	7	8	9
10	11	12	13	14	15	16
17	18	19	20	21	22	23
24	25	26	27	28	29	30

JUL (31)
SUN	MON	TUE	WED	THU	FRI	SAT
1	2	3	4	5	6	7
8	9	10	11	12	13	14
15	16	17	18	19	20	21
22	23	24	25	26	27	28
29	30	31				

AUG (32)
SUN	MON	TUE	WED	THU	FRI	SAT
			1	2	3	4
5	6	7	8	9	10	11
12	13	14	15	16	17	18
19	20	21	22	23	24	25
26	27	28	29	30	31	

SEP (33)
SUN	MON	TUE	WED	THU	FRI	SAT
						1
2	3	4	5	6	7	8
9	10	11	12	13	14	15
16	17	18	19	20	21	22
23/30	24	25	26	27	28	29

OCT (34)
SUN	MON	TUE	WED	THU	FRI	SAT
	1	2	3	4	5	6
7	8	9	10	11	12	13
14	15	16	17	18	19	20
21	22	23	24	25	26	27
28	29	30	31			

NOV (35)
SUN	MON	TUE	WED	THU	FRI	SAT
				1	2	3
4	5	6	7	8	9	10
11	12	13	14	15	16	17
18	19	20	21	22	23	24
25	26	27	28	29	30	

DEC (36)
SUN	MON	TUE	WED	THU	FRI	SAT
						1
2	3	4	5	6	7	8
9	10	11	12	13	14	15
16	17	18	19	20	21	22
23/30	24/31	25	26	27	28	29

MARCH 21
(37)

JUNE 21
(38)

SEPT. 21
(39)

DEC. 21
(40)

JUNE 5 — TIM!
(41)

MARCH 2 — ANNIVERSARY
(42)

JULY 4 — INDEPENDENCE DAY / STATE BANK / CLOSED - JULY 4
(43)

APRIL 4 — EASTER SUNDAY
(44)

MAY 17 — DOCTOR 4:30
(45)

AUGUST
(46)

Months of the year

25. January

26. February

27. March

28. April

29. May

30. June

31. July

32. August

33. September

34. October

35. November

36. December

Seasons

37. spring

38. summer

39. fall

40. winter

41. birthday

42. anniversary

43. legal holiday

44. religious holiday

45. appointment

46. vacation

Use the new language.

Look at the **ordinal numbers** on page **14**.

Use ordinal numbers to say the date.

It's _June 5th_. It's _the fifth_.

Talk about your birthday.

My birthday is in the winter.

My birthday is in January.

My birthday is on January twenty-sixth.

Money

Coins

1. $.01 = 1¢
a penny/1 cent

2. $.05 = 5¢
a nickel/5 cents

3. $.10 = 10¢
a dime/10 cents

4. $.25 = 25¢
a quarter/25 cents

5. $.50 = 50¢
a half dollar

6. $1.00
a silver dollar

Bills

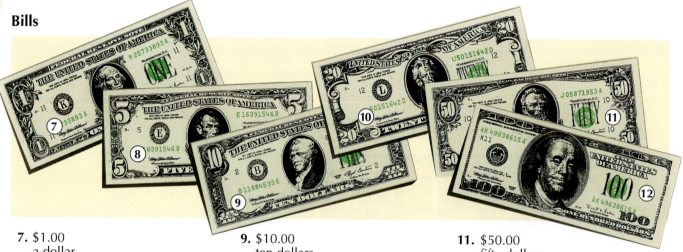

7. $1.00
a dollar

8. $5.00
five dollars

9. $10.00
ten dollars

10. $20.00
twenty dollars

11. $50.00
fifty dollars

12. $100.00
one hundred dollars

Ways to pay

13. cash

14. personal check

15. credit card

16. money order

17. traveler's check

More vocabulary

borrow: to get money from someone and return it later
lend: to give money to someone and get it back later
pay back: to return the money that you borrowed

Other ways to talk about money:

a *dollar bill* or *a one*
a *five-dollar bill* or *a five*

a *ten-dollar bill* or *a ten*
a *twenty-dollar bill* or *a twenty*

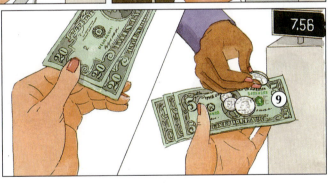

A. shop for	**E. keep**	2. regular price	6. price/cost
B. sell	**F. return**	3. sale price	7. sales tax
C. pay for / **buy**	**G. exchange**	4. bar code	8. total
D. give	1. price tag	5. receipt	9. change

More vocabulary

When you use a credit card to shop, you get a **bill** in the mail. Bills list, in writing, the items you bought and the total you have to pay.

Share your answers.

1. Name three things you pay for every month.
2. Name one thing you will buy this week.
3. Where do you like to shop?

Age and Physical Description

1. children

2. baby

3. toddler

4. 6-year-old boy

5. 10-year-old girl

6. teenagers

7. 13-year-old boy

8. 19-year-old girl

9. adults

10. woman

11. man

12. senior citizen

13. young

14. middle-aged

15. elderly

16. tall

17. average height

18. short

19. pregnant

20. heavyset

21. average weight

22. thin/slim

23. attractive

24. cute

25. physically challenged

26. sight impaired/blind

27. hearing impaired/deaf

Talk about yourself and your teacher.

I am young, average height, and average weight.

My teacher is a middle-aged, tall, thin man.

Use the new language.

Turn to **Hobbies and Games,** pages **162–163.**

Describe each person on the page.

He's a heavyset, short, senior citizen.

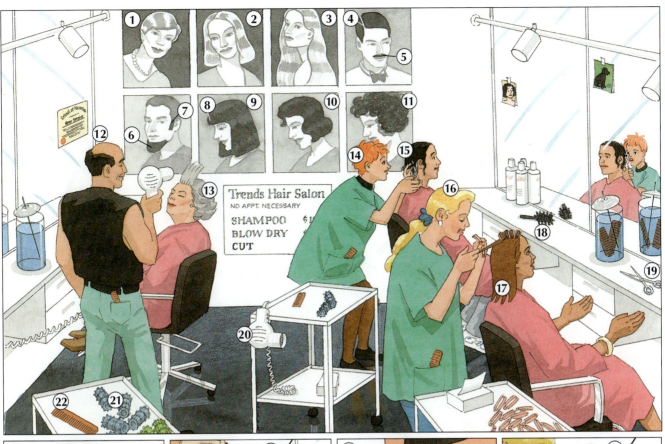

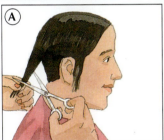
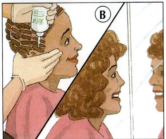
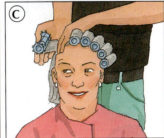
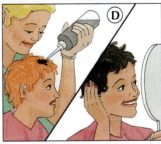

1. short hair	8. bangs	15. black hair	22. comb
2. shoulder-length hair	9. straight hair	16. blond hair	**A. cut** hair
3. long hair	10. wavy hair	17. brown hair	**B. perm** hair
4. part	11. curly hair	18. brush	**C. set** hair
5. mustache	12. bald	19. scissors	**D. color** hair/**dye** hair
6. beard	13. gray hair	20. blow dryer	
7. sideburns	14. red hair	21. rollers	

More vocabulary

hair stylist: a person who cuts, sets, and perms hair

hair salon: the place where a hair stylist works

Talk about your hair.

My hair is <u>long</u>, <u>straight</u>, and <u>brown</u>.

I have <u>long</u>, <u>straight</u>, <u>brown</u> hair.

When I was a child my hair was <u>short</u>, <u>curly</u>, and <u>blond</u>.

Tom Lee's Family

1. grandparents

Min

Lu

2. grandmother

3. grandfather

4. parents

Rose

Chang

Helen

Daniel

5. mother

6. father

10. aunt

11. uncle

Tom

Lily

Alex

Emily

8. sister

9. brother

12. cousin

7. (Min and Lu's) grandson

Berta

Mario

Ana Garcia's Family

13. mother-in-law

14. father-in-law

Ana

Marta

Carlos

Tito

20. (Tito's) wife

15. sister-in-law

16. brother-in-law

19. husband

Alice

Eddie

Sara

Felix

17. niece

18. nephew

21. daughter

22. son

More vocabulary

Lily and Emily are Min and Lu's **granddaughters**.

Daniel is Min and Lu's **son-in-law**.

Ana is Berta and Mario's **daughter-in-law**.

Share your answers.

1. How many brothers and sisters do you have?
2. What number son or daughter are you?
3. Do you have any children?

Lisa Smith's Family

23. married

Carol   Dan

Lisa

24. divorced

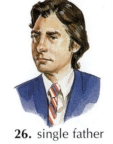

25. single mother

26. single father

Rick   Carol

27. remarried

Dan   Sue

Rick   Carol

28. stepfather

David   Mary

29. half brother   **30.** half sister

Lisa

Dan   Sue

31. stepmother

Kim   Bill

32. stepsister   **33.** stepbrother

More vocabulary

Carol is Dan's **former wife**.

Sue is Dan's **wife**.

Dan is Carol's **former husband**.

Rick is Carol's **husband**.

Lisa is the **stepdaughter** of both Rick and Sue.

Daily Routines

6:00 A.M.

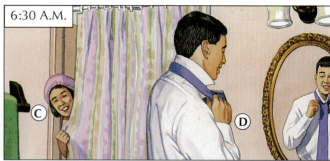

6:30 A.M.

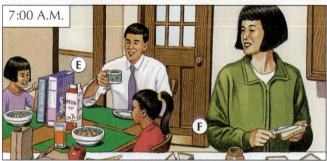

7:00 A.M.

7:30 A.M.

8:00 A.M.

10:00 A.M.

4:30 P.M.

5:00 P.M.

A. **wake up**

B. **get up**

C. **take** a shower

D. **get dressed**

E. **eat** breakfast

F. **make** lunch

G. **take** the children to school

H. **take** the bus to school

I. **drive** to work/**go** to work

J. **be** in school

K. **work**

L. **go** to the market

M. **leave** work

Grammar point: 3rd person singular

For **he** and **she**, we add **-s** or **-es** to the verb.

He/She wakes up.

He/She watches TV.

These verbs are different (irregular):

be   *He/She is in school at 10:00 a.m.*

have   *He/She has dinner at 6:30 p.m.*

5:30 P.M. N O

6:00 P.M. P Q

6:30 P.M. R

7:30 P.M. S T

8:00 P.M. U V

8:30 P.M. W

10:30 P.M. X

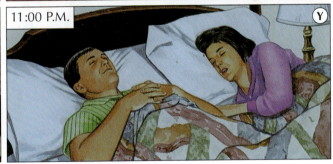

11:00 P.M. Y

N. clean the house

O. pick up the children

P. cook dinner

Q. come home / **get** home

R. have dinner

S. watch TV

T. do homework

U. relax

V. read the paper

W. exercise

X. go to bed

Y. go to sleep

Talk about your daily routine.

I take a shower in the morning.
I go to school in the evening.
I go to bed at 11 o'clock.

Share your answers.

1. Who makes dinner in your family?
2. Who goes to the market?
3. Who goes to work?

Life Events

A. **be born**

B. **start** school

C. **immigrate**

D. **graduate**

E. **learn** to drive

F. **join** the army

G. **get** a job

H. **become** a citizen

I. **rent** an apartment

J. **go** to college

K. **fall in love**

L. **get married**

Grammar point: past tense

start	
learn	
join	+ed
rent	
travel	

immigrate	
graduate	
move	+d
retire	
die	

These verbs are different (irregular):

be	— was	have	— had
get	— got	buy	— bought
become	— became		
go	— went		
fall	— fell		

1960

1967

M. have a baby

N. travel

1971

STATE BANK

1971

ABC MOVERS

O. buy a house

P. move

1985

1997

Q. have a grandchild

R. die

Registro Civil
Acta de Nacimiento

MARTÍN PEREZ DE LEÓN
01-05-25
JOSÉ PEREZ
RITA LEÓN

1

Los Angeles High School

Martin Perez

Rachid Hababi
Josephine R. Klee
Loretta Sommers

2

RESIDENT ALIEN
US Department of Justice-
Immigration and Naturalization Service
PEREZ, MARTIN
01-05-25
B043398414
10-28-40
Martin Perez

3

1. birth certificate

2. diploma

3. Resident Alien card

DMV **CALIFORNIA** DMV
DRIVER LICENSE
MO6178   CLASS: C
EXPIRES: XI-IX-IX
PEREZ, MARTIN
Martin Perez

4

SOCIAL SECURITY
987-65-4321
PEREZ, MARTIN
Martin Perez

5

THE UNITED STATES OF AMERICA
No. 20779079
Certificate of Naturalization
INS Registration No. B04 398 414
Martin Perez
Henrietta J. Mulholland

6

4. driver's license

5. Social Security card

6. Certificate of Naturalization

California State University
CSU
Martin Perez
Bachelor of Science
June 1964
With Honors
Sigmund G. Kaufmann

7

MAY 24 1955
CERTIFICATE of REGISTRY of MARRIAGE

MARTIN	LEON	PEREZ	D1-0
ROSA	MARIA	LOPEZ	11

8

PASSPORT
UNITED STATES OF AMERICA
PASSPORT
USA   PEREZ, MARTIN
01-05-25X   01-1
779876543   43-5-33
1-2-67

9

7. college degree

8. marriage license

9. passport

More vocabulary

When a husband dies, his wife becomes a **widow**.

When a wife dies, her husband becomes a **widower**.

When older people stop working, we say they **retire**.

Talk about yourself.

I was born in 1968.

I learned to drive in 1987.

I immigrated in 1990.

1. hot

2. thirsty

3. sleepy

4. cold

5. hungry

6. full

7. comfortable

8. uncomfortable

9. disgusted

10. calm

11. nervous

12. in pain

13. worried

14. sick

15. well

16. relieved

17. hurt

18. lonely

19. in love

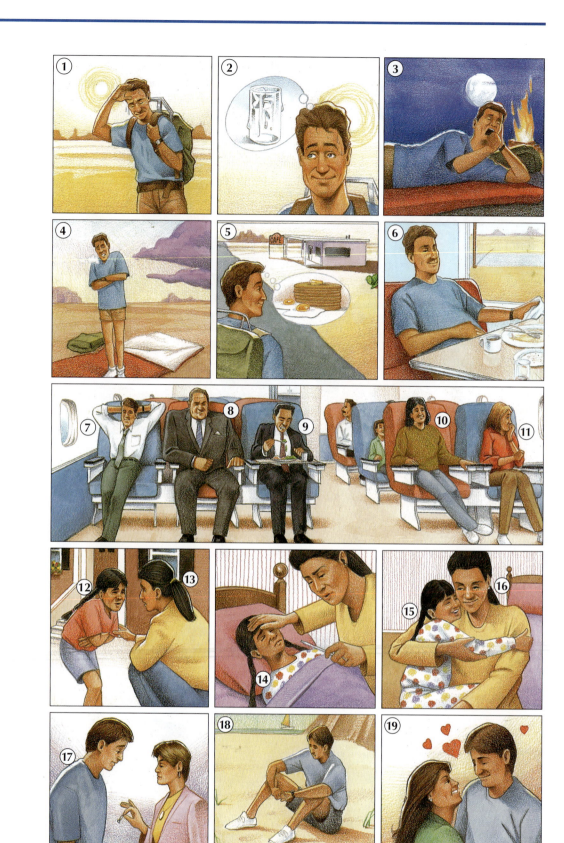

More vocabulary
furious: very angry
terrified: very scared
overjoyed: very happy

exhausted: very tired
starving: very hungry
humiliated: very embarrassed

Talk about your feelings.
I feel <u>happy</u> when I see <u>my friends</u>.
I feel <u>homesick</u> when I think about <u>my family</u>.

20. sad

21. homesick

22. proud

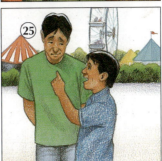

23. excited

24. scared

25. embarrassed

26. bored

27. confused

28. frustrated

29. angry

30. upset

31. surprised

32. happy

33. tired

Use the new language.

Look at **Clothing I,** page **64,** and answer the questions.

1. How does the runner feel?

2. How does the man at the bus stop feel?

3. How does the woman at the bus stop feel?

4. How do the teenagers feel?

5. How does the little boy feel?

A Graduation

The Ceremony

1. graduating class
2. gown
3. cap
4. stage

5. podium
6. graduate
7. diploma
8. valedictorian

9. guest speaker
10. audience
11. photographer
A. **graduate**

B. **applaud / clap**
C. **cry**
D. **take** a picture
E. **give** a speech

Talk about what the people in the pictures are doing.

She is [tak**ing** a picture.
*giv**ing** a speech.*
*smil**ing**.*
*laugh**ing**.*

He is [mak**ing** a toast.
*clap**ping**.*

They are [graduat**ing**.
*hug**ging**.*
*kiss**ing**.*
*applaud**ing**.*

32

The Party

12. caterer	**15.** banner	**18.** gifts	**H. laugh**
13. buffet	**16.** dance floor	**F. kiss**	**I. make a toast**
14. guests	**17.** DJ (disc jockey)	**G. hug**	**J. dance**

Share your answers.

1. Did you ever go to a graduation? Whose?

2. Did you ever give a speech? Where?

3. Did you ever hear a great speaker? Where?

4. Did you ever go to a graduation party?

5. What do you like to eat at parties?

6. Do you like to dance at parties?

Places to Live

1. the city/an urban area   2. the suburbs   3. a small town   4. the country/a rural area

5. apartment building

6. house

7. townhouse

8. mobile home

9. college dormitory

10. shelter

11. nursing home

12. ranch

13. farm

More vocabulary

duplex house: a house divided into two homes

condominium: an apartment building where each apartment is owned separately

co-op: an apartment building owned by the residents

Share your answers.

1. Do you like where you live?
2. Where did you live in your country?
3. What types of housing are there near your school?

Renting an apartment

A. **look for** a new apartment

B. **talk** to the manager

C. **sign** a rental agreement

D. **move in**

E. **unpack**

F. **pay** the rent

Buying a house

G. **talk** to the Realtor

H. **make** an offer

I. **get** a loan

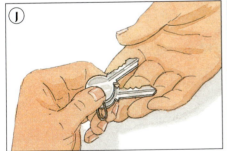

J. **take** ownership

K. **arrange** the furniture

L. **pay** the mortgage

More vocabulary

lease: a rental agreement for a specific period of time
utilities: gas, water, and electricity for the home

Practice talking to an apartment manager.

How much is the rent?
Are utilities included?
When can I move in?

Entrance

Laundry Room

Recreation Room

Garage

1. first floor

2. second floor

3. third floor

4. fourth floor

5. roof garden

6. playground

7. fire escape

8. intercom/speaker

9. security system

10. doorman

11. vacancy sign

12. manager/superintendent

13. security gate

14. storage locker

15. parking space

More vocabulary

rec room: a short way of saying **recreation room**

basement: the area below the street level of an apartment or a house

Talk about where you live.

I live in Apartment 3 near the entrance.

I live in Apartment 11 on the second floor near the fire escape.

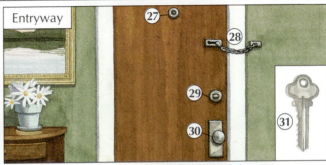

16. swimming pool	**23.** fire exit	**30.** doorknob
17. balcony	**24.** trash chute	**31.** key
18. courtyard	**25.** smoke detector	**32.** landlord
19. air conditioner	**26.** stairway	**33.** tenant
20. trash bin	**27.** peephole	**34.** elevator
21. alley	**28.** door chain	**35.** stairs
22. neighbor	**29.** dead-bolt lock	**36.** mailboxes

Grammar point: *there is, there are*

singular: *there is*   plural: *there are*

There is a fire exit in the hallway.

There are mailboxes in the lobby.

Talk about apartments.

My apartment has an elevator, a lobby, and a rec room.

My apartment doesn't have a pool or a garage.

My apartment needs air conditioning.

1. floor plan
2. backyard
3. fence
4. mailbox
5. driveway
6. garage

7. garage door
8. screen door
9. porch light
10. doorbell
11. front door
12. storm door

13. steps
14. front walk
15. front yard
16. deck
17. window
18. shutter

19. gutter
20. roof
21. chimney
22. TV antenna

More vocabulary
two-story house: a house with two floors
downstairs: the bottom floor
upstairs: the part of a house above the bottom floor

Share your answers.
1. What do you like about this house?
2. What's something you don't like about the house?
3. Describe the perfect house.

1. hedge	**8.** sprinkler	**15.** pruning shears	**22.** lawn mower
2. hammock	**9.** hose	**16.** wheelbarrow	**A.** **weed** the flower bed
3. garbage can	**10.** compost pile	**17.** watering can	**B.** **water** the plants
4. leaf blower	**11.** rake	**18.** flowerpot	**C.** **mow** the lawn
5. patio furniture	**12.** hedge clippers	**19.** flower	**D.** **plant** a tree
6. patio	**13.** shovel	**20.** bush	**E.** **trim** the hedge
7. barbecue grill	**14.** trowel	**21.** lawn	**F.** **rake** the leaves

Talk about your yard and gardening.

I like to <u>plant trees</u>.

I don't like to <u>weed</u>.

I like/don't like to work in the yard/garden.

Share your answers.

1. What flowers, trees, or plants do you see in the picture? (Look at **Trees, Plants, and Flowers,** pages **128–129** for help.)

2. Do you ever use a barbecue grill to cook?

A Kitchen

1. cabinet	**8.** shelf	**15.** toaster oven	**22.** counter
2. paper towels	**9.** refrigerator	**16.** pot	**23.** drawer
3. dish drainer	**10.** freezer	**17.** teakettle	**24.** pan
4. dishwasher	**11.** coffeemaker	**18.** stove	**25.** electric mixer
5. garbage disposal	**12.** blender	**19.** burner	**26.** food processor
6. sink	**13.** microwave oven	**20.** oven	**27.** cutting board
7. toaster	**14.** electric can opener	**21.** broiler	

Talk about the location of kitchen items.

The toaster oven is *on the counter* *near the stove.*
The microwave is *above the stove.*

Share your answers.

1. Do you have a garbage disposal? a dishwasher? a microwave?

2. Do you eat in the kitchen?

1. china cabinet	**8.** candlestick	**15.** pepper shaker	**22.** knife
2. set of dishes	**9.** vase	**16.** dining room chair	**23.** spoon
3. platter	**10.** tray	**17.** dining room table	**24.** plate
4. ceiling fan	**11.** teapot	**18.** tablecloth	**25.** bowl
5. light fixture	**12.** sugar bowl	**19.** napkin	**26.** glass
6. serving dish	**13.** creamer	**20.** place mat	**27.** coffee cup
7. candle	**14.** saltshaker	**21.** fork	**28.** mug

Practice asking for things in the dining room.

Please pass the platter.

May I have the creamer?

Could I have a fork, please?

Share your answers.

1. What are the women in the picture saying?

2. In your home, where do you eat?

3. Do you like to make dinner for your friends?

A Living Room

1. bookcase
2. basket
3. track lighting
4. lightbulb
5. ceiling
6. wall
7. painting

8. mantel
9. fireplace
10. fire
11. fire screen
12. logs
13. wall unit
14. stereo system

15. floor lamp
16. drapes
17. window
18. plant
19. sofa / couch
20. throw pillow
21. end table

22. magazine holder
23. coffee table
24. armchair / easy chair
25. love seat
26. TV (television)
27. carpet

Use the new language.
Look at **Colors**, page **12**, and describe this room.
There is a gray sofa and a gray armchair.

Talk about your living room.
In my living room I have a sofa, two chairs, and a coffee table.
I don't have a fireplace or a wall unit.

1. hamper	**8.** towel rack	**15.** toilet paper	**22.** sink
2. bathtub	**9.** tile	**16.** toilet brush	**23.** soap
3. rubber mat	**10.** showerhead	**17.** toilet	**24.** soap dish
4. drain	**11.** (mini)blinds	**18.** mirror	**25.** wastebasket
5. hot water	**12.** bath towel	**19.** medicine cabinet	**26.** scale
6. faucet	**13.** hand towel	**20.** toothbrush	**27.** bath mat
7. cold water	**14.** washcloth	**21.** toothbrush holder	

More vocabulary

half bath: a bathroom without a shower or bathtub

linen closet: a closet or cabinet for towels and sheets

stall shower: a shower without a bathtub

Share your answers.

1. Do you turn off the water when you brush your teeth? wash your hair? shave?

2. Does your bathroom have a bathtub or a stall shower?

A Bedroom

1. mirror	**8.** bed	**15.** headboard	**22.** dust ruffle
2. dresser/bureau	**9.** pillow	**16.** clock radio	**23.** rug
3. drawer	**10.** pillowcase	**17.** lamp	**24.** floor
4. closet	**11.** bedspread	**18.** lampshade	**25.** mattress
5. curtains	**12.** blanket	**19.** light switch	**26.** box spring
6. window shade	**13.** flat sheet	**20.** outlet	**27.** bed frame
7. photograph	**14.** fitted sheet	**21.** night table	

Use the new language.

Describe this room. (See **Describing Things**, page **11,** for help.)

I see a soft pillow and a beautiful bedspread.

Share your answers.

1. What is your favorite thing in your bedroom?

2. Do you have a clock in your bedroom? Where is it?

3. Do you have a mirror in your bedroom? Where is it?

1. bunk bed	**7.** bumper pad	**13.** diaper pail	**19.** cradle
2. comforter	**8.** chest of drawers	**14.** dollhouse	**20.** coloring book
3. night-light	**9.** baby monitor	**15.** blocks	**21.** crayons
4. mobile	**10.** teddy bear	**16.** ball	**22.** puzzle
5. wallpaper	**11.** smoke detector	**17.** picture book	**23.** stuffed animals
6. crib	**12.** changing table	**18.** doll	**24.** toy chest

Talk about where items are in the room.

The dollhouse is near _the coloring book_.

The teddy bear is on _the chest of drawers_.

Share your answers.

1. Do you think this is a good room for children? Why?

2. What toys did you play with when you were a child?

3. What children's stories do you know?

A. dust the furniture	**G.** make the bed	**M.** wash the dishes
B. recycle the newspapers	**H.** put away the toys	**N.** dry the dishes
C. clean the oven	**I.** vacuum the carpet	**O.** wipe the counter
D. wash the windows	**J.** mop the floor	**P.** change the sheets
E. sweep the floor	**K.** polish the furniture	**Q.** take out the garbage
F. empty the wastebasket	**L.** scrub the floor	

Talk about yourself.

I wash <u>the dishes</u> every day.
I change <u>the sheets</u> every week.
I never <u>dry the dishes</u>.

Share your answers.

1. Who does the housework in your family?
2. What is your favorite cleaning job?
3. What is your least favorite cleaning job?

1. feather duster

2. recycling bin

3. oven cleaner

4. rubber gloves

5. steel-wool soap pads

6. rags

7. stepladder

8. glass cleaner

9. squeegee

10. broom

11. dustpan

12. trash bags

13. vacuum cleaner

14. vacuum cleaner attachments

15. vacuum cleaner bag

16. wet mop

17. dust mop

18. furniture polish

19. scrub brush

20. bucket/pail

21. dishwashing liquid

22. dish towel

23. cleanser

24. sponge

Practice asking for the items.

I want to <u>*wash the windows*</u>.
Please hand me <u>*the squeegee*</u>.

I have to <u>*sweep the floor*</u>.
Can you get me <u>*the broom*</u>, *please?*

1. The water heater is **not working**.

2. The power is **out**.

3. The roof is **leaking**.

4. The wall is **cracked**.

5. The window is **broken**.

6. The lock is **broken**.

7. The steps are **broken**.

8. roofer

9. electrician

10. repair person

11. locksmith

12. carpenter

13. fuse box

14. gas meter

Use the new language.
Look at **Tools and Building Supplies,** pages **150–151.**
Name the tools you use for household repairs.

I use a hammer and nails to fix a broken step.
I use a wrench to repair a dripping faucet.

15. The furnace is **broken**.

16. The faucet is **dripping**.

17. The sink is **overflowing**.

18. The toilet is **stopped up**.

19. The pipes are **frozen**.

20. plumber

21. exterminator

Household pests

22. termite(s)

23. flea(s)

24. ant(s)

25. cockroach(es)

26. mice*

27. rat(s)

*Note: *one mouse, two mice*

More vocabulary

fix: to repair something that is broken

exterminate: to kill household pests

pesticide: a chemical that is used to kill household pests

Share your answers.

1. Who does household repairs in your home?

2. What is the worst problem a home can have?

3. What is the most expensive problem a home can have?

1. grapes	**9.** grapefruit	**17.** strawberries	**25.** dates
2. pineapples	**10.** oranges	**18.** raspberries	**26.** prunes
3. bananas	**11.** lemons	**19.** blueberries	**27.** raisins
4. apples	**12.** limes	**20.** papayas	**28.** not ripe
5. peaches	**13.** tangerines	**21.** mangoes	**29.** ripe
6. pears	**14.** avocadoes	**22.** coconuts	**30.** rotten
7. apricots	**15.** cantaloupes	**23.** nuts	
8. plums	**16.** cherries	**24.** watermelons	

Language note: *a bunch of*
We say *a bunch of grapes* and *a bunch of bananas.*

Share your answers.

1. Which fruits do you put in a fruit salad?

2. Which fruits are sold in your area in the summer?

3. What fruits did you have in your country?

1. lettuce	**9.** celery	**17.** scallions	**25.** string beans
2. cabbage	**10.** parsley	**18.** eggplants	**26.** mushrooms
3. carrots	**11.** spinach	**19.** peas	**27.** corn
4. zucchini	**12.** cucumbers	**20.** artichokes	**28.** onions
5. radishes	**13.** squash	**21.** potatoes	**29.** garlic
6. beets	**14.** turnips	**22.** yams	
7. sweet peppers	**15.** broccoli	**23.** tomatoes	
8. chili peppers	**16.** cauliflower	**24.** asparagus	

Language note: *a bunch of, a head of*

We say *a bunch of carrots, a bunch of celery,* and *a bunch of spinach.*

We say *a head of lettuce, a head of cabbage,* and *a head of cauliflower.*

Share your answers.

1. Which vegetables do you eat raw? cooked?
2. Which vegetables need to be in the refrigerator?
3. Which vegetables don't need to be in the refrigerator?

Meat and Poultry

Beef

1. roast beef
2. steak
3. stewing beef
4. ground beef

5. beef ribs
6. veal cutlets
7. liver
8. tripe

Pork

9. ham
10. pork chops
11. bacon
12. sausage

Lamb

13. lamb shanks
14. leg of lamb
15. lamb chops

16. chicken
17. turkey
18. duck

19. breasts
20. wings
21. thighs

22. drumsticks
23. gizzards

24. **raw** chicken
25. **cooked** chicken

More vocabulary
vegetarian: a person who doesn't eat meat
Meat and poultry without bones are called **boneless**.
Poultry without skin is called **skinless**.

Share your answers.
1. What kind of meat do you eat most often?
2. What kind of meat do you use in soup?
3. What part of the chicken do you like the most?

1. white bread
2. wheat bread
3. rye bread
4. smoked turkey
5. salami

6. pastrami
7. roast beef
8. corned beef
9. American cheese
10. cheddar cheese

11. Swiss cheese
12. jack cheese
13. potato salad
14. coleslaw
15. pasta salad

Fish

16. trout
17. catfish
18. whole salmon
19. salmon steak

20. halibut
21. filet of sole

Shellfish

22. crab
23. lobster
24. shrimp
25. scallops

26. mussels
27. oysters
28. clams
29. **fresh** fish
30. **frozen** fish

Practice ordering a sandwich.

I'd like roast beef and American cheese on rye bread.
Tell what you want on it.
Please put tomato, lettuce, onions, and mustard on it.

Share your answers.
1. Do you like to eat fish?
2. Do you buy fresh or frozen fish?

The Market

1. bottle return	**3.** shopping cart	**6.** baked goods	**9.** dairy section
2. meat and poultry section	**4.** canned goods	**7.** shopping basket	**10.** pet food
	5. aisle	**8.** manager	**11.** produce section

24. soup	**28.** rice	**32.** cake	**36.** butter
25. tuna	**29.** bread	**33.** yogurt	**37.** sour cream
26. beans	**30.** rolls	**34.** eggs	**38.** cheese
27. spaghetti	**31.** cookies	**35.** milk	**39.** margarine

12. frozen foods

13. baking products

14. paper products

15. beverages

16. snack foods

17. checkstand

18. cash register

19. checker

20. line

21. bagger

22. paper bag

23. plastic bag

40. potato chips

41. candy bar

42. gum

43. frozen vegetables

44. ice cream

45. flour

46. spices

47. cake mix

48. sugar

49. oil

50. apple juice

51. instant coffee

52. soda

53. bottled water

54. plastic wrap

55. aluminum foil

Containers and Packaged Foods

 ①

 ②

 ③

 ④

 ⑤

 ⑥

1. bottle   **2.** jar   **3.** can   **4.** carton   **5.** container   **6.** box

 ⑦

 ⑧

 ⑨

 ⑩

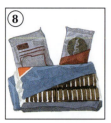 ⑪

 ⑫

7. bag   **8.** package   **9.** six-pack   **10.** loaf   **11.** roll   **12.** tube

 ⑬

 ⑭

 ⑮

 ⑯

 ⑰

 ⑱

 ⑲

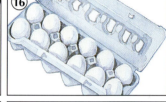 ⑳

 ㉑

 ㉒

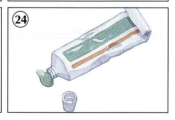 ㉓

㉔

13. a bottle of soda   **17.** a container of cottage cheese   **21.** a six-pack of soda

14. a jar of jam   **18.** a box of cereal   **22.** a loaf of bread

15. a can of soup   **19.** a bag of flour   **23.** a roll of paper towels

16. a carton of eggs   **20.** a package of cookies   **24.** a tube of toothpaste

Grammar point: *How much? How many?*
Some foods can be counted: *one apple, two apples.*
How many apples do you need? *I need **two** apples.*

Some foods cannot be counted, like liquids, grains, spices, or dairy foods. For these, count containers: *one box of rice, two boxes of rice.*
How much rice do you need? *I need **two boxes.***

56

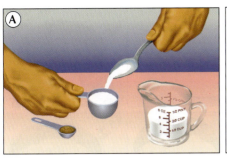

A. Measure the ingredients.

B. Weigh the food.

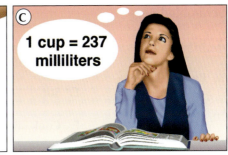

1 cup = 237 milliliters

C. Convert the measurements.

Liquid measures

1 fl. oz.   1 c.   1 pt.   1 qt.   1 gal.

Dry measures

1 tsp.   1 TBS.   1/4 c.   1/2 c.   1 c.

Weight

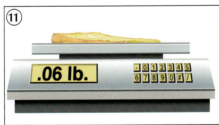 

.06 lb.   1.00 lb.

1. a fluid ounce of water

2. a cup of oil

3. a pint of yogurt

4. a quart of milk

5. a gallon of apple juice

6. a teaspoon of salt

7. a tablespoon of sugar

8. a 1/4 cup of brown sugar

9. a 1/2 cup of raisins

10. a cup of flour

11. an ounce of cheese

12. a pound of roast beef

VOLUME
1 fl. oz. = 30 milliliters (ml.)
1 c. = 237 ml.
1 pt. = .47 liters (l.)
1 qt. = .95 l.
1 gal. = 3.79 l.

EQUIVALENCIES

3 tsp. = 1 TBS.	2 c. = 1 pt.
2 TBS. = 1 fl. oz.	2 pt. = 1 qt.
8 fl. oz. = 1 c.	4 qt. = 1 gal.

WEIGHT
1 oz. = 28.35 grams (g.)
1 lb. = 453.6 g.
2.205 lbs. = 1 kilogram
1 lb. = 16 oz.

Food Preparation

Scrambled eggs

A. **Break** 3 eggs.

B. **Beat** well.

C. **Grease** the pan.

D. **Pour** the eggs into the pan.

E. **Stir.**

F. **Cook** until done.

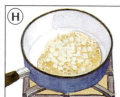

Vegetable casserole

G. **Chop** the onions.

H. **Sauté** the onions.

I. **Steam** the broccoli.

J. **Grate** the cheese.

K. **Mix** the ingredients.

L. **Bake** at 350° for 45 minutes.

Chicken soup

M. **Cut up** the chicken.

N. **Peel** the carrots.

O. **Slice** the carrots.

P. **Boil** the chicken.

Q. **Add** the vegetables.

R. **Simmer** for 1 hour.

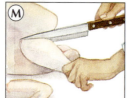

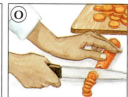

Five ways to cook chicken

S. fry

T. barbecue / grill

U. roast

V. broil

W. stir-fry

Talk about the way you prepare these foods.

I *fry* eggs.

I *bake* potatoes.

Share your answers.

1. What are popular ways in your country to make rice? vegetables? meat?

2. What is your favorite way to cook chicken?

58

1. can opener

2. grater

3. plastic storage container

4. steamer

5. frying pan

6. pot

7. ladle

8. double boiler

9. wooden spoon

10. garlic press

11. casserole dish

12. carving knife

13. roasting pan

14. roasting rack

15. vegetable peeler

16. paring knife

17. colander

18. kitchen timer

19. spatula

20. eggbeater

21. whisk

22. strainer

23. tongs

24. lid

25. saucepan

26. cake pan

27. cookie sheet

28. pie pan

29. pot holders

30. rolling pin

31. mixing bowl

Talk about how to use the utensils.

You use a peeler to peel potatoes.

You use a pot to cook soup.

Use the new language.

Look at **Food Preparation**, page 58.

Name the different utensils you see.

Fast Food

1. hamburger	8. green salad	15. doughnut	22. sugar substitute
2. french fries	9. taco	16. salad bar	23. ketchup
3. cheeseburger	10. nachos	17. lettuce	24. mustard
4. soda	11. frozen yogurt	18. salad dressing	25. mayonnaise
5. iced tea	12. milk shake	19. booth	26. relish
6. hot dog	13. counter	20. straw	A. eat
7. pizza	14. muffin	21. sugar	B. drink

More vocabulary

donut: doughnut (spelling variation)

condiments: relish, mustard, ketchup, mayonnaise, etc.

Share your answers.

1. What would you order at this restaurant?
2. Which fast foods are popular in your country?
3. How often do you eat fast food? Why?

Breakfast

Lunch

Dinner

Desserts

Beverages

1. scrambled eggs

2. sausage

3. toast

4. waffles

5. syrup

6. pancakes

7. bacon

8. grilled cheese sandwich

9. chef's salad

10. soup of the day

11. mashed potatoes

12. roast chicken

13. steak

14. baked potato

15. pasta

16. garlic bread

17. fried fish

18. rice pilaf

19. cake

20. pudding

21. pie

22. coffee

23. decaf coffee

24. tea

Practice ordering from the menu.

I'd like a grilled cheese sandwich and some soup.

I'll have the chef's salad and a cup of decaf coffee.

Use the new language.

Look at **Fruit,** page **50.**

Order a slice of pie using the different fruit flavors.

Please give me a slice of apple pie.

1. hostess

2. dining room

3. menu

4. server/waiter

5. patron/diner

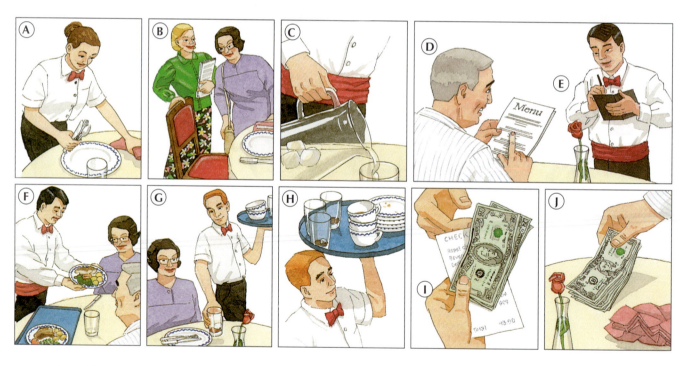

A. **set** the table

B. **seat** the customer

C. **pour** the water

D. **order** from the menu

E. **take** the order

F. **serve** the meal

G. **clear** the table

H. **carry** the tray

I. **pay** the check

J. **leave** a tip

More vocabulary

eat out: to go to a restaurant to eat

take out: to buy food at a restaurant and take it home to eat

Practice giving commands.

Please <u>set the table</u>.

I'd like you to <u>clear the table</u>.

It's time to <u>serve the meal</u>.

6. server / waitress	**8.** bread basket	**10.** kitchen	**12.** dishroom
7. dessert tray	**9.** busperson	**11.** chef	**13.** dishwasher

  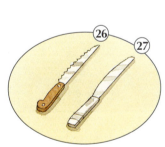 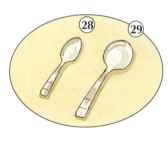

14. place setting	**18.** soup bowl	**22.** saucer	**26.** steak knife
15. dinner plate	**19.** water glass	**23.** napkin	**27.** knife
16. bread-and-butter plate	**20.** wine glass	**24.** salad fork	**28.** teaspoon
17. salad plate	**21.** cup	**25.** dinner fork	**29.** soupspoon

Talk about how you set the table in your home.

The glass is on the right.
The fork goes on the left.
The napkin is next to the plate.

Share your answers.

1. Do you know anyone who works in a restaurant? What does he or she do?

2. In your opinion, which restaurant jobs are hard? Why?

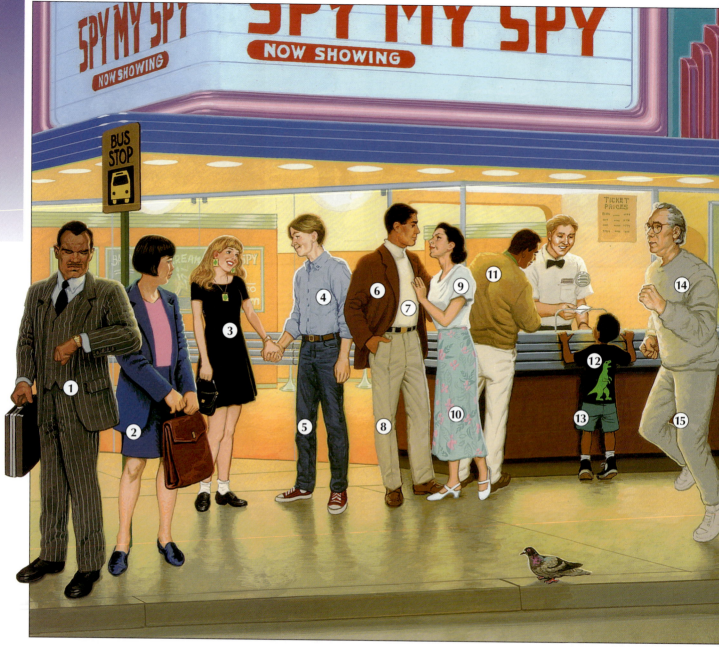

1. three-piece suit	**6.** sports coat	**11.** pullover sweater
2. suit	**7.** turtleneck	**12.** T-shirt
3. dress	**8.** slacks/pants	**13.** shorts
4. shirt	**9.** blouse	**14.** sweatshirt
5. jeans	**10.** skirt	**15.** sweatpants

More vocabulary:

outfit: clothes that look nice together

When clothes are popular, they are **in fashion.**

Talk about what you're wearing today and what you wore yesterday.

I'm wearing a gray sweater, a red T-shirt, and blue jeans.

Yesterday I wore a green pullover sweater, a white shirt, and black slacks.

16. jumpsuit

17. uniform

18. jumper

19. maternity dress

20. knit shirt

21. overalls

22. tunic

23. leggings

24. vest

25. split skirt

26. sports shirt

27. cardigan sweater

28. tuxedo

29. evening gown

Use the new language.

Look at **A Graduation,** pages **32–33.**

Name the clothes you see.

The man at the podium is wearing a suit.

Share your answers.

1. Which clothes in this picture are in fashion now?

2. Who is the best-dressed person in this line? Why?

3. What do you wear when you go to the movies?

1. hat	**5.** gloves	**8.** parka	**12.** earmuffs
2. overcoat	**6.** cap	**9.** mittens	**13.** down vest
3. leather jacket	**7.** jacket	**10.** ski cap	**14.** ski mask
4. wool scarf/muffler		**11.** tights	**15.** down jacket

16. umbrella	**20.** trench coat	**24.** windbreaker
17. raincoat	**21.** sunglasses	**25.** cover-up
18. poncho	**22.** swimming trunks	**26.** swimsuit/bathing suit
19. rain boots	**23.** straw hat	**27.** baseball cap

Use the new language.

Look at **Weather,** page **10.**

Name the clothing for each weather condition.

Wear a jacket when it's windy.

Share your answers.

1. Which is better in the rain, an umbrella or a poncho?

2. Which is better in the cold, a parka or a down jacket?

3. Do you have more summer clothes or winter clothes?

1. leotard **3.** bike shorts   **4.** pajamas   **7.** blanket sleeper

2. tank top   **5.** nightgown   **8.** bathrobe

                6. slippers   **9.** nightshirt

10. undershirt   **16.** (bikini) panties   **22.** full slip

11. long underwear   **17.** briefs / underpants   **23.** half slip

12. boxer shorts   **18.** girdle   **24.** knee-highs

13. briefs   **19.** garter belt   **25.** kneesocks

14. athletic supporter / jockstrap   **20.** bra   **26.** stockings

15. socks   **21.** camisole   **27.** pantyhose

More vocabulary

lingerie: underwear or sleepwear for women

loungewear: clothing (sometimes sleepwear) people wear around the home

Share your answers.

1. What do you wear when you exercise?

2. What kind of clothing do you wear for sleeping?

Shoes and Accessories

1. salesclerk

2. suspenders

3. shoe department

4. silk scarves*

5. hats

12. sole

13. heel

14. shoelace

15. toe

16. pumps

17. high heels

18. boots

19. loafers

20. oxfords

21. hiking boots

22. tennis shoes

23. athletic shoes

24. sandals

*Note: one scarf, two scarves

Talk about the shoes you're wearing today.

I'm wearing a pair of <u>white sandals</u>.

Practice asking a salesperson for help.

Could I try on these <u>sandals</u> in size <u>10</u>?

Do you have any <u>silk scarves</u>?

Where are <u>the hats</u>?

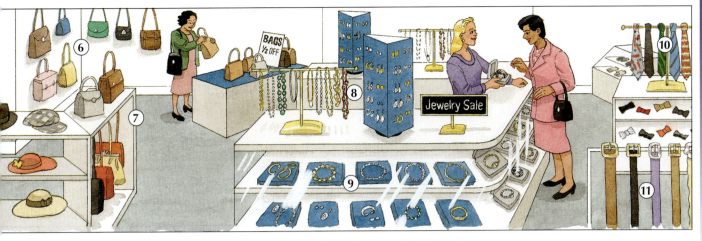

6. purses / handbags

7. display case

8. jewelry

9. necklaces

10. ties

11. belts

25. change purse

26. wallet

27. shoulder bag

28. backpack / bookbag

29. tote bag

30. string of pearls

31. chain

32. beads

33. locket

34. (wrist)watch

35. bracelet

36. pin

37. pierced earrings

38. clip-on earrings

39. ring

40. bow tie

41. belt buckle

42. handkerchief

43. key chain

Share your answers.

1. Which of these accessories are usually worn by women? by men?

2. Which of these do you wear every day?

3. Which of these would you wear to a job interview? Why?

4. Which accessory would you like to receive as a present? Why?

Describing Clothes

Sizes

1. extra small   **2.** small   **3.** medium   **4.** large   **5.** extra large

Patterns

| **6.** solid green | **8.** polka-dotted | **10.** print | **12.** floral |
| **7.** striped | **9.** plaid | **11.** checked | **13.** paisley |

Types of material

14. wool sweater   **16. cotton** T-shirt   **18. leather** boots

15. silk scarf   **17. linen** jacket   **19. nylon** stockings*

Problems

20. too small   **22.** stain   **24. broken** zipper

21. too big   **23.** rip / tear   **25. missing** button

*Note: Nylon, polyester, rayon, and plastic are synthetic materials.

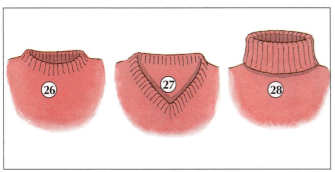

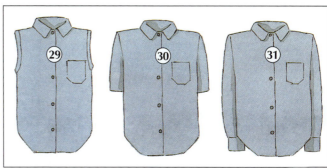

26. **crewneck** sweater

27. **V-neck** sweater

28. **turtleneck** sweater

29. **sleeveless** shirt

30. **short-sleeved** shirt

31. **long-sleeved** shirt

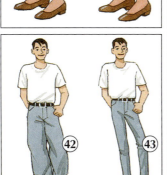

32. **new** shoes

33. **old** shoes

34. **long** skirt

35. **short** skirt

36. **formal** dress

37. **casual** dress

38. **plain** blouse

39. **fancy** blouse

40. **light** jacket

41. **heavy** jacket

42. **loose** pants / **baggy** pants

43. **tight** pants

44. **wide** tie

45. **narrow** tie

46. **low** heels

47. **high** heels

Talk about yourself.

I like <u>long-sleeved</u> shirts and <u>baggy</u> pants.
I like <u>short skirts</u> and <u>high heels</u>.
I usually wear <u>plain</u> clothes.

Share your answers.

1. What type of material do you usually wear in the summer? in the winter?

2. What patterns do you see around you?

3. Are you wearing casual or formal clothes?

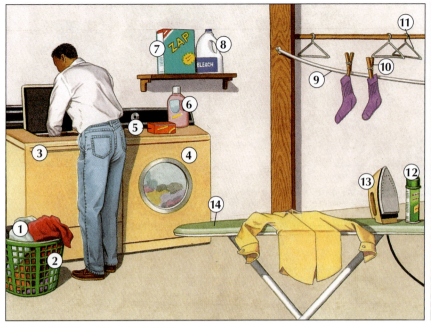

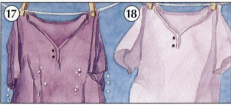

1. laundry	**6.** fabric softener	**11.** hanger	**16.** **clean** T-shirt
2. laundry basket	**7.** laundry detergent	**12.** spray starch	**17.** **wet** T-shirt
3. washer	**8.** bleach	**13.** iron	**18.** **dry** T-shirt
4. dryer	**9.** clothesline	**14.** ironing board	**19.** **wrinkled** shirt
5. dryer sheets	**10.** clothespin	**15.** **dirty** T-shirt	**20.** **ironed** shirt

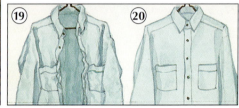

A. **Sort** the laundry.	**D.** **Clean** the lint trap.	**G.** **Iron** the clothes.
B. **Add** the detergent.	**E.** **Unload** the dryer.	**H.** **Hang up** the clothes.
C. **Load** the washer.	**F.** **Fold** the laundry.	

More vocabulary

dry cleaners: a business that cleans clothes using chemicals, not water and detergent

 wash in cold water only

 no bleach

 line dry

 dry-clean only, do not wash

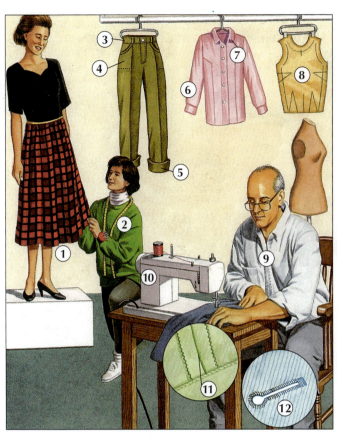

A. **sew** by hand

B. **sew** by machine

C. lengthen

D. shorten

E. take in

F. let out

1. hemline	**4.** pocket	**7.** collar	**10.** sewing machine
2. dressmaker	**5.** cuff	**8.** pattern	**11.** seam
3. waistband	**6.** sleeve	**9.** tailor	**12.** buttonhole

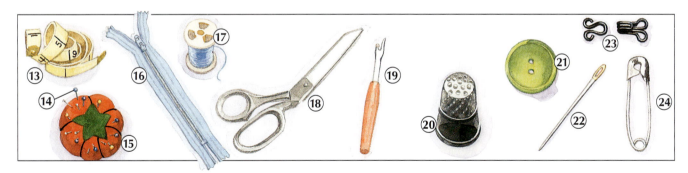

13. tape measure	**16.** zipper	**19.** seam ripper	**22.** needle
14. pin	**17.** spool of thread	**20.** thimble	**23.** hook and eye
15. pin cushion	**18.** (pair of) scissors	**21.** button	**24.** safety pin

More vocabulary

pattern maker: a person who makes patterns

garment worker: a person who works in a clothing factory

fashion designer: a person who makes original clothes

Share your answers.

1. Do you know how to use a sewing machine?

2. Can you sew by hand?

The Body

1. head	**7.** foot	**13.** chest
2. neck	**8.** hand	**14.** breast
3. abdomen	**9.** arm	**15.** elbow
4. waist	**10.** shoulder	**16.** thigh
5. hip	**11.** back	**17.** knee
6. leg	**12.** buttocks	**18.** calf

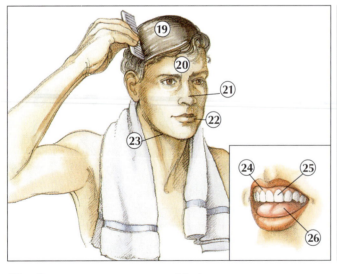

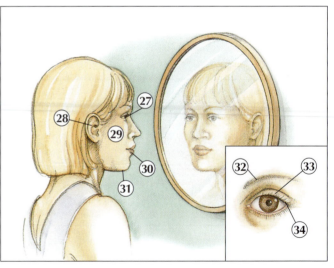

The face	**23.** jaw	**27.** eye	**32.** eyebrow
19. hair	**24.** gums	**28.** ear	**33.** eyelid
20. forehead	**25.** teeth	**29.** cheek	**34.** eyelashes
21. nose	**26.** tongue	**30.** lip	
22. mouth		**31.** chin	

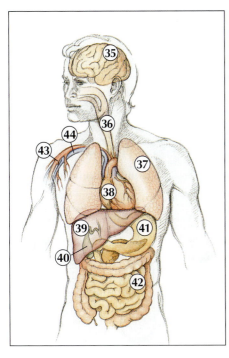

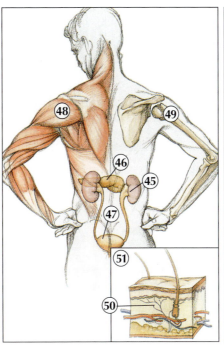

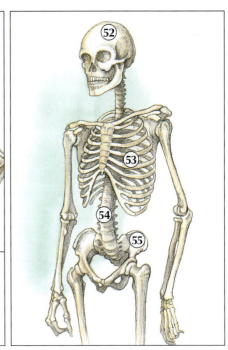

Inside the body

35. brain

36. throat

37. lung

38. heart

39. liver

40. gallbladder

41. stomach

42. intestines

43. artery

44. vein

45. kidney

46. pancreas

47. bladder

48. muscle

49. bone

50. nerve

51. skin

The skeleton

52. skull

53. rib cage

54. spinal column

55. pelvis

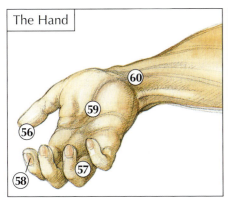

The Hand

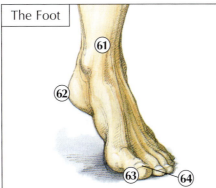

The Foot

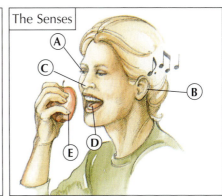

The Senses

56. thumb

57. fingers

58. fingernail

59. palm

60. wrist

61. ankle

62. heel

63. toe

64. toenail

A. **see**

B. **hear**

C. **smell**

D. **taste**

E. **touch**

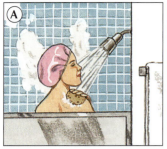

A. take a shower

B. bathe / take a bath

C. use deodorant

D. put on sunscreen

1. shower cap

2. soap

3. bath powder / talcum powder

4. deodorant

5. perfume / cologne

6. sunscreen

7. body lotion

8. moisturizer

E. wash…hair

F. rinse…hair

G. comb…hair

H. dry…hair

I. brush…hair

9. shampoo

10. conditioner

11. hair gel

12. hair spray

13. comb

14. brush

15. curling iron

16. blow dryer

17. hair clip

18. barrette

19. bobby pins

J. brush…teeth

K. floss…teeth

L. gargle

M. shave

20. toothbrush

21. toothpaste

22. dental floss

23. mouthwash

24. electric shaver

25. razor

26. razor blade

27. shaving cream

28. aftershave

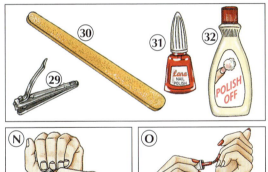

N. cut…nails

O. polish…nails

P. put on…makeup

29. nail clipper

30. emery board

31. nail polish

32. nail polish remover

33. eyebrow pencil

34. eye shadow

35. eyeliner

36. blush / rouge

37. lipstick

38. mascara

39. face powder

40. foundation

More vocabulary

A product without perfume or scent is **unscented.**

A product that is better for people with allergies is **hypoallergenic.**

Share your answers.

1. What is your morning routine if you stay home? if you go out?

2. Do women in your culture wear makeup? How old are they when they begin to use it?

Symptoms and Injuries

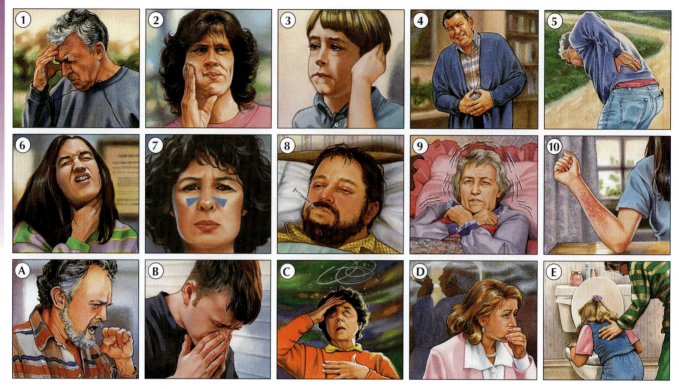

1. headache	**6.** sore throat	**A.** **cough**
2. toothache	**7.** nasal congestion	**B.** **sneeze**
3. earache	**8.** fever/temperature	**C.** **feel** dizzy
4. stomachache	**9.** chills	**D.** **feel** nauseous
5. backache	**10.** rash	**E.** **throw up/vomit**

     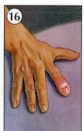  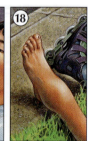

11. insect bite	**14.** sunburn	**17.** **bloody** nose
12. bruise	**15.** blister	**18.** **sprained** ankle
13. cut	**16.** **swollen** finger	

Use the new language.

Look at **Health Care,** pages **80–81.**

Tell what medication or treatment you would use for each health problem.

Share your answers.

1. For which problems would you go to a doctor? use medication? do nothing?

2. What do you do for a sunburn? for a headache?

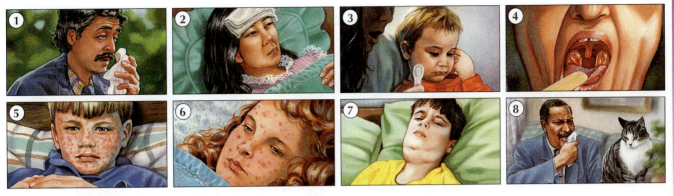

Common illnesses and childhood diseases

1. cold

2. flu

3. ear infection

4. strep throat

5. measles

6. chicken pox

7. mumps

8. allergies

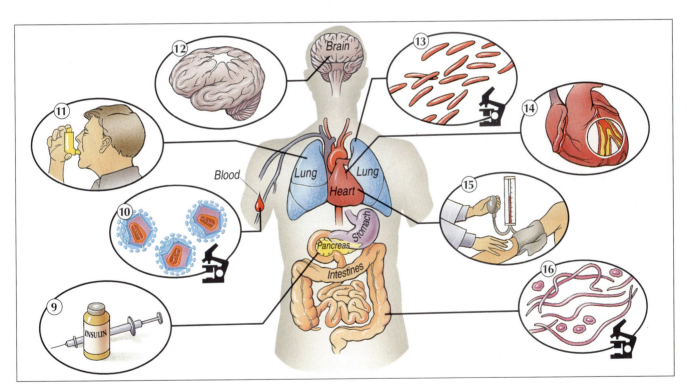

Medical conditions and serious diseases

9. diabetes

10. HIV (human immunodeficiency virus)

11. asthma

12. brain cancer

13. TB (tuberculosis)

14. heart disease

15. high blood pressure

16. intestinal parasites

More vocabulary

AIDS (acquired immunodeficiency syndrome): a medical condition that results from contracting the HIV virus

influenza: flu

hypertension: high blood pressure

infectious disease: a disease that is spread through air or water

Share your answers.

Which diseases on this page are infectious?

79

Health Care

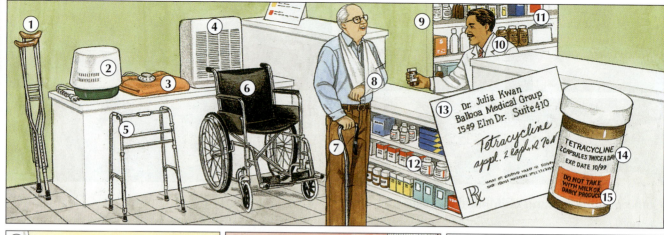

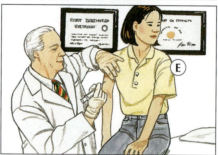

1. crutches

2. humidifier

3. heating pad

4. air purifier

5. walker

6. wheelchair

7. cane

8. sling

9. pharmacy

10. pharmacist

11. prescription medication

12. over-the-counter medication

13. prescription

14. prescription label

15. warning label

A. **Get** bed rest.

B. **Drink** fluids.

C. **Change** your diet.

D. **Exercise.**

E. **Get** an injection.

F. **Take** medicine.

More vocabulary

dosage: how much medicine you take and how many times a day you take it

expiration date: the last day the medicine can be used

treatment: something you do to get better

Staying in bed, drinking fluids, and getting physical therapy are treatments.

An injection that stops a person from getting a serious disease is called **an immunization** or **a vaccination.**

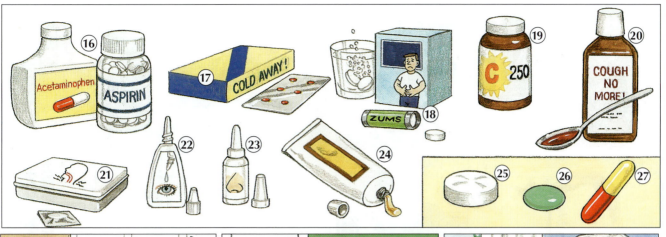

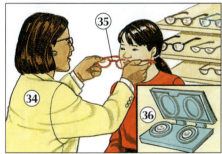

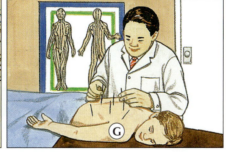

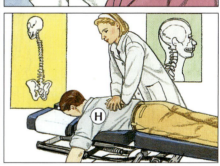

16. pain reliever

17. cold tablets

18. antacid

19. vitamins

20. cough syrup

21. throat lozenges

22. eyedrops

23. nasal spray

24. ointment

25. tablet

26. pill

27. capsule

28. orthopedist

29. cast

30. physical therapist

31. brace

32. audiologist

33. hearing aid

34. optometrist

35. (eye)glasses

36. contact lenses

G. Get acupuncture.

H. Go to a chiropractor.

Share your answers.

1. What's the best treatment for a headache? a sore throat? a stomachache? a fever?

2. Do you think vitamins are important? Why or why not?

3. What treatments are popular in your culture?

 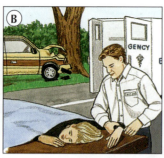  

   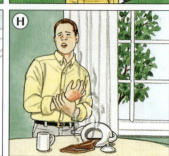

  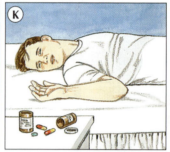 

A. be injured / be hurt

B. be unconscious

C. be in shock

D. have a heart attack

E. have an allergic reaction

F. get an electric shock

G. get frostbite

H. burn (your)self

I. drown

J. swallow poison

K. overdose on drugs

L. choke

M. bleed

N. can't breathe

O. fall

P. break a bone

Grammar point: past tense

burn	— burned	choke	— choked	bleed	— bled
drown	— drowned	be	— was, were	can't	— couldn't
swallow	— swallowed	have	— had	fall	— fell
overdose	— overdosed	get	— got	break	— broke

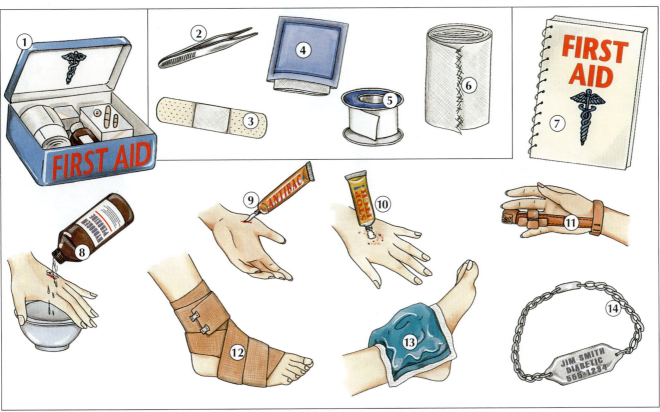

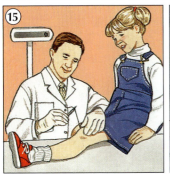
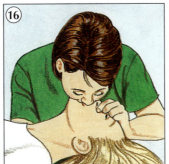
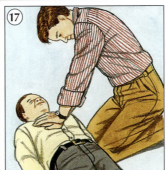

1. first aid kit

2. tweezers

3. adhesive bandage

4. sterile pad

5. tape

6. gauze

7. first aid manual

8. hydrogen peroxide

9. antibacterial ointment

10. antihistamine cream

11. splint

12. elastic bandage

13. ice pack

14. medical emergency bracelet

15. stitches

16. rescue breathing

17. CPR (cardiopulmonary resuscitation)

18. Heimlich maneuver

Important Note: Only people who are properly trained should give stitches or do CPR.

Share your answers.

1. Do you have a First Aid kit in your home? Where can you buy one?

2. When do you use hydrogen peroxide? an elastic support bandage? antihistamine cream?

3. Do you know first aid? Where did you learn it?

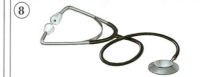

Medical clinic

1. waiting room
2. receptionist
3. patient
4. insurance card
5. insurance form

6. doctor
7. scale
8. stethoscope
9. examining room
10. nurse

11. eye chart
12. blood pressure gauge
13. examination table
14. syringe
15. thermometer

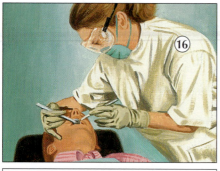

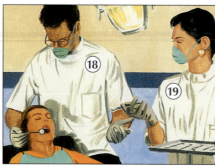

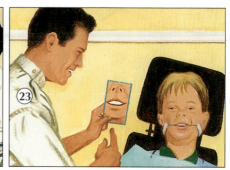

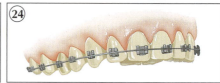

Dental clinic

16. dental hygienist
17. tartar
18. dentist

19. dental assistant
20. cavity
21. drill

22. filling
23. orthodontist
24. braces

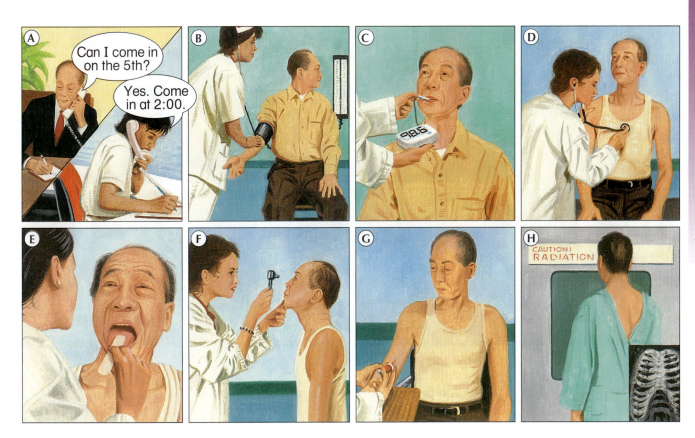

A. **make** an appointment

B. **check**…blood pressure

C. **take**…temperature

D. **listen** to…heart

E. **look** in…throat

F. **examine**…eyes

G. **draw**…blood

H. **get** an X ray

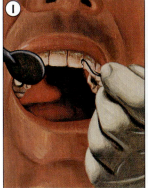

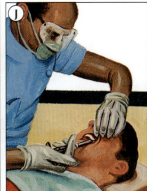

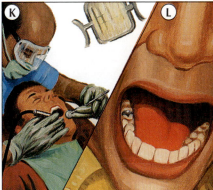

I. **clean**…teeth

J. **give**…a shot of anesthetic

K. **drill** a tooth

L. **fill** a cavity

M. **pull** a tooth

More vocabulary

get a checkup: to go for a medical exam

extract a tooth: to pull out a tooth

Share your answers.

1. What is the average cost of a medical exam in your area?

2. Some people are nervous at the dentist's office. What can they do to relax?

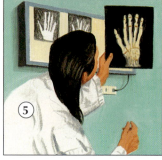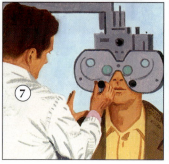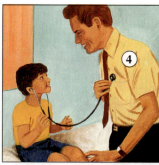

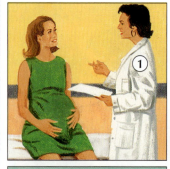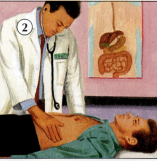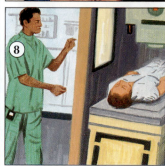

Hospital staff

1. obstetrician

2. internist

3. cardiologist

4. pediatrician

5. radiologist

6. psychiatrist

7. ophthalmologist

8. X-ray technician

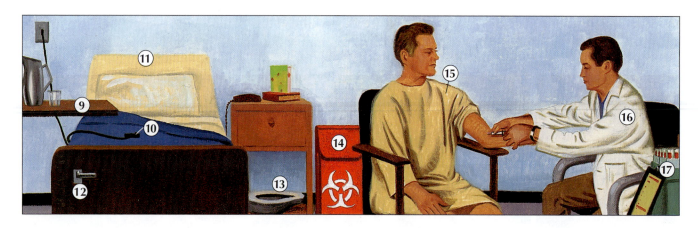

Patient's room

9. bed table

10. call button

11. hospital bed

12. bed control

13. bedpan

14. medical waste disposal

15. hospital gown

16. lab technician

17. blood work/blood test

More vocabulary

nurse practitioner: a nurse licensed to give medical exams

specialist: a doctor who only treats specific medical problems

gynecologist: a specialist who examines and treats women

nurse midwife: a nurse practitioner who examines pregnant women and delivers babies

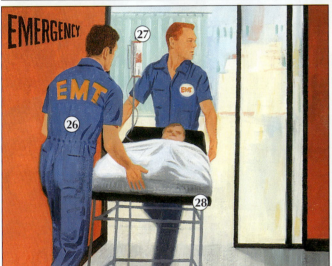

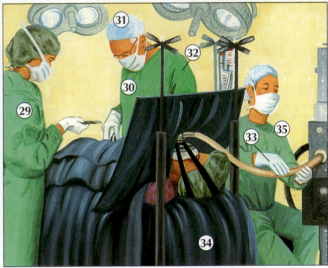

Nurse's station

18. orderly

19. volunteer

20. medical charts

21. vital signs monitor

22. RN (registered nurse)

23. medication tray

24. LPN (licensed practical nurse)/ LVN (licensed vocational nurse)

25. dietician

Emergency room

26. emergency medical technician (EMT)

27. IV (intravenous drip)

28. stretcher/gurney

Operating room

29. surgical nurse

30. surgeon

31. surgical cap

32. surgical gown

33. latex gloves

34. operating table

35. anesthesiologist

Practice asking for the hospital staff.

Please get the nurse. I have a question for her.
Where's the anesthesiologist? I need to talk to her.
I'm looking for the lab technician. Have you seen him?

Share your answers.

1. Have you ever been to an emergency room? Who helped you?

2. Have you ever been in the hospital? How long did you stay?

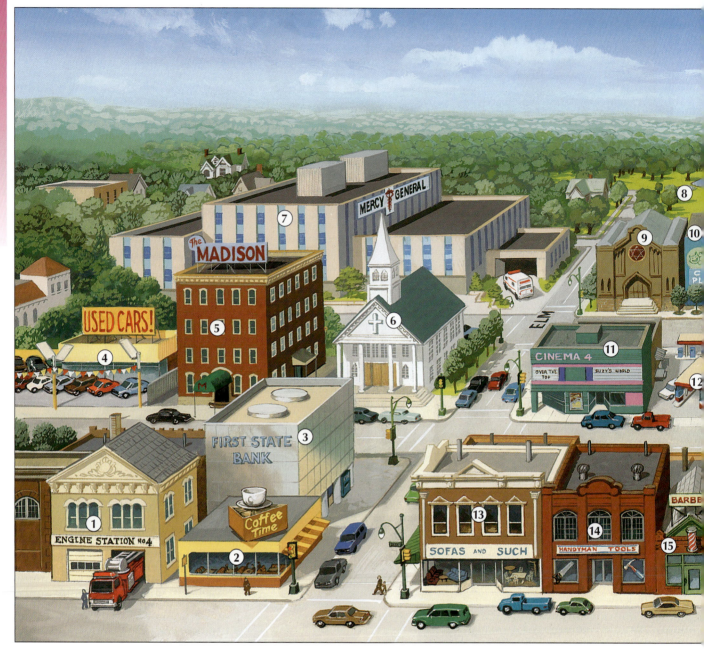

1. fire station	**6.** church	**11.** movie theater
2. coffee shop	**7.** hospital	**12.** gas station
3. bank	**8.** park	**13.** furniture store
4. car dealership	**9.** synagogue	**14.** hardware store
5. hotel	**10.** theater	**15.** barber shop

More vocabulary

skyscraper: a very tall office building

downtown/city center: the area in a city with the city hall, courts, and businesses

Practice giving your destination.

I'm going to go <u>downtown</u>.

I have to go to <u>the post office</u>.

16. bakery

17. city hall

18. courthouse

19. police station

20. market

21. health club

22. motel

23. mosque

24. office building

25. high-rise building

26. parking garage

27. school

28. library

29. post office

Practice asking for and giving the locations of buildings.

Where's the post office?

  It's on Oak Street.

Share your answers.

1. Which of the places in this picture do you go to every week?

2. Is it good to live in a city? Why or why not?

3. What famous cities do you know?

1. Laundromat

2. drugstore / pharmacy

3. convenience store

4. photo shop

5. parking space

6. traffic light

7. pedestrian

8. crosswalk

9. street

10. curb

11. newsstand

12. mailbox

13. drive-thru window

14. fast food restaurant

15. bus

A. **cross** the street

B. **wait** for the light

C. **drive** a car

More vocabulary

neighborhood: the area close to your home

do errands: to make a short trip from your home to buy or pick up something

Talk about where to buy things.

You can buy newspapers at a newsstand.

You can buy donuts at a donut shop.

You can buy food at a convenience store.

16. bus stop	**22.** copy center / print shop	**28.** fire hydrant
17. corner	**23.** streetlight	**29.** sign
18. parking meter	**24.** dry cleaners	**30.** street vendor
19. motorcycle	**25.** nail salon	**31.** cart
20. donut shop	**26.** sidewalk	**D.** **park** the car
21. public telephone	**27.** garbage truck	**E.** **ride** a bicycle

Share your answers.

1. Do you like to do errands?

2. Do you always like to go to the same stores?

3. Which businesses in the picture are also in your neighborhood?

4. Do you know someone who has a small business? What kind?

5. What things can you buy from a street vendor?

1. music store

2. jewelry store

3. candy store

4. bookstore

5. toy store

6. pet store

7. card store

8. optician

9. travel agency

10. shoe store

11. fountain

12. florist

More vocabulary

beauty shop: hair salon

men's store: a store that sells men's clothing

dress shop: a store that sells women's clothing

Talk about where you want to shop in this mall.

Let's go to the card store.

I need to buy a card for Maggie's birthday.

13. department store	**17.** maternity shop	**21.** escalator
14. food court	**18.** electronics store	**22.** information booth
15. video store	**19.** directory	
16. hair salon	**20.** ice cream stand	

Practice asking for and giving the location of different shops.

Where's <u>the maternity shop</u>?

  It's on <u>the first floor</u>, next to <u>the hair salon.</u>

Share your answers.

1. Do you like shopping malls? Why or why not?

2. Some people don't go to the mall to shop. Name some other things you can do in a mall.

A Childcare Center

1. parent

2. stroller

3. childcare worker

4. cubby

5. toys

6. rocking chair

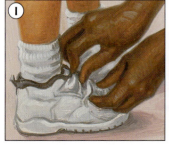

A. **drop off**

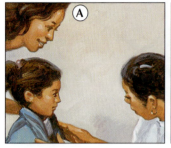

B. **hold**

C. **nurse**

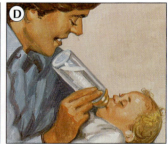

D. **feed**

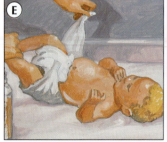

E. **change** diapers

F. **read** a story

G. **pick up**

H. **rock**

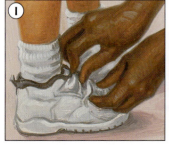

I. **tie** shoes

J. **dress**

K. **play**

L. **take** a nap

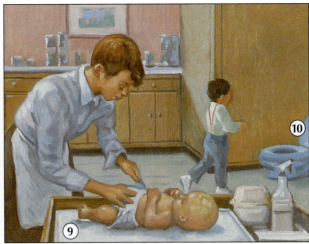

7. high chair   **8.** bib   **9.** changing table   **10.** potty seat

11. playpen

12. walker

13. car safety seat

14. baby carrier

15. baby backpack

16. carriage

17. wipes

18. baby powder

19. disinfectant

20. disposable diapers

21. cloth diapers

22. diaper pins

23. diaper pail

24. training pants

25. formula

26. bottle

27. nipple

28. baby food

29. pacifier

30. teething ring

31. rattle

U.S. Mail

1. envelope
2. letter
3. postcard
4. greeting card
5. package

6. letter carrier
7. return address
8. mailing address
9. postmark
10. stamp / postage

11. certified mail
12. priority mail
13. air letter / aerogramme
14. ground post / parcel post
15. Express Mail / overnight mail

Emily Rose
1543 Oak Lane
Springvale, CA 91254
⑦

SPRINGVALE
5-7-99
CA
⑨

USA
⑩

Alyson Shepard
249 Courtney Drive
Newton, NY 10043
⑧

FRAGILE ⑭

EXPRESS MAIL
UNITED STATES POSTAL SERVICE ⑮

A. **address** a postcard

B. **send** it / **mail** it

C. **deliver** it

D. **receive** it

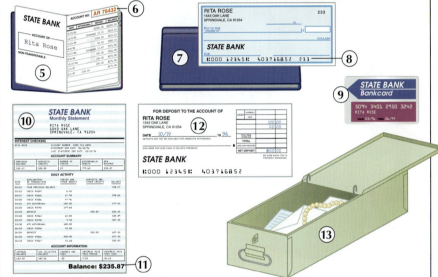

1. teller
2. vault
3. ATM (automated teller machine)
4. security guard

5. passbook
6. savings account number
7. checkbook
8. checking account number
9. ATM card
10. monthly statement
11. balance
12. deposit slip
13. safe-deposit box

Using the ATM machine

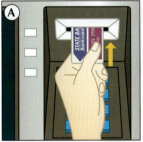

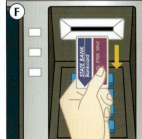

A. **Insert** your ATM card.
B. **Enter** your PIN number.*
C. **Make** a deposit.
D. **Withdraw** cash.
E. **Transfer** funds.
F. **Remove** your ATM card.

*PIN: personal identification number

More vocabulary

overdrawn account: When there is not enough money in an account to pay a check, we say the account is overdrawn.

Share your answers.

1. Do you use a bank?
2. Do you use an ATM card?
3. Name some things you can put in a safe-deposit box.

1. reference librarian	**7.** magazine	**13.** videocassette	**19.** library card
2. reference desk	**8.** newspaper	**14.** CD (compact disc)	**20.** library book
3. atlas	**9.** online catalog	**15.** record	**21.** title
4. microfilm reader	**10.** card catalog	**16.** checkout desk	**22.** author
5. microfilm	**11.** media section	**17.** library clerk	
6. periodical section	**12.** audiocassette	**18.** encyclopedia	

More vocabulary

check a book out: to borrow a book from the library

nonfiction: real information, history or true stories

fiction: stories from the author's imagination

Share your answers.

1. Do you have a library card?

2. Do you prefer to buy books or borrow them from the library?

A. **arrest** a suspect

B. **hire** a lawyer/**hire** an attorney

C. **appear** in court

1. police officer

2. handcuffs

3. guard

4. defense attorney

5. defendant

6. judge

D. **stand trial**

7. courtroom

8. jury

9. evidence

10. prosecuting attorney

11. witness

12. court reporter

13. bailiff

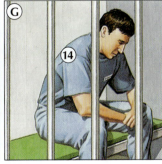

E. **give** the verdict*

F. **sentence** the defendant

G. **go** to jail/**go** to prison

H. **be released**

14. convict

*Note: There are two possible verdicts, "guilty" and "not guilty."

Share your answers.

1. What are some differences between the legal system in the United States and the one in your country?

2. Do you want to be on a jury? Why or why not?

1. vandalism

2. gang violence

3. drunk driving

4. illegal drugs

5. mugging

6. burglary

7. assault

8. murder

9. gun

More vocabulary

commit a crime: to do something illegal

criminal: someone who commits a crime

victim: someone who is hurt or killed by someone else

Share your answers.

1. Is there too much crime on TV? in the movies?

2. Do you think people become criminals from watching crime on TV?

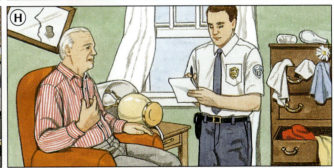

A. Walk with a friend.

B. Stay on well-lit streets.

C. Hold your purse close to your body.

D. Protect your wallet.

E. Lock your doors.

F. Don't open your door to strangers.

G. Don't drink and **drive**.

H. Report crimes to the police.

More vocabulary

Neighborhood Watch: a group of neighbors who watch for criminals in their neighborhood

designated drivers: people who don't drink alcoholic beverages so that they can drive drinkers home

Share your answers.

1. Do you feel safe in your neighborhood?

2. Look at the pictures. Which of these things do you do?

3. What other things do you do to stay safe?

Emergencies and Natural Disasters

1. lost child

2. car accident

3. airplane crash

4. explosion

5. earthquake

6. mudslide

7. fire

8. firefighter

9. fire truck

Practice reporting a fire.

This is <u>Lisa Broad</u>. There is a fire.

The address is <u>323 Oak Street.</u>

Please send someone quickly.

Share your answers.

1. Can you give directions to your home if there is a fire?

2. What information do you give to the other driver if you are in a car accident?

10. drought

11. blizzard

12. hurricane

13. tornado

14. volcanic eruption

15. tidal wave

16. flood

17. search and rescue team

Share your answers.

1. Which disasters are common in your area? Which never happen?

2. What can you do to prepare for emergencies?

3. Do you have emergency numbers near your telephone?

4. What organizations will help you in an emergency?

1. bus stop	**7.** passenger	**13.** train station	**19.** taxi stand
2. route	**8.** bus driver	**14.** ticket	**20.** taxi driver
3. schedule	**9.** subway	**15.** platform	**21.** meter
4. bus	**10.** track	**16.** conductor	**22.** taxi license
5. fare	**11.** token	**17.** train	**23.** ferry
6. transfer	**12.** fare card	**18.** taxi/cab	

More vocabulary

hail a taxi: to get a taxi driver's attention by raising your hand

miss the bus: to arrive at the bus stop late

Talk about how you and your friends come to school.

I take the bus to school.
You take the train.
We take the subway.

He drives to school.
She walks to school.
They ride bikes.

1. **under** the bridge

2. **over** the bridge

3. **across** the water

4. **into** the taxi

5. **out of** the taxi

6. **onto** the highway

7. **off** the highway

8. **down** the stairs

9. **up** the stairs

10. **around** the corner

11. **through** the tunnel

Grammar point: *into, out of, on, off*

We say, *get **into** a taxi or a car.*

But we say, *get **on** a bus, a train, or a plane.*

We say, *get **out of** a taxi or a car.*

But we say, *get **off** a bus, a train, or a plane.*

Cars and Trucks

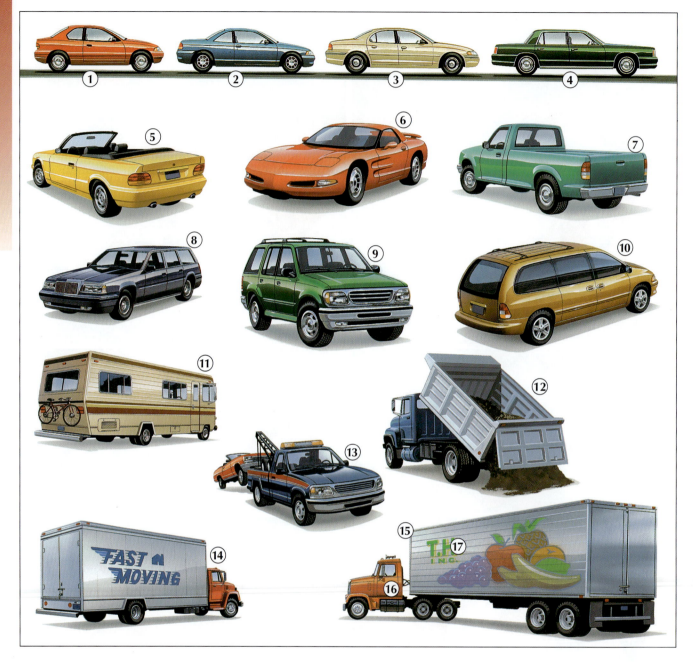

1. subcompact	**6.** sports car	**10.** minivan
2. compact	**7.** pickup truck	**11.** camper
3. midsize car	**8.** station wagon	**12.** dump truck
4. full-size car	**9.** SUV (sports utility vehicle)	**13.** tow truck
5. convertible		**14.** moving van

15. tractor trailer / semi

16. cab

17. trailer

More vocabulary

make: the name of the company that makes the car

model: the style of car

Share your answers.

1. What is your favorite kind of car?

2. What kind of car is good for a big family? for a single person?

Directions

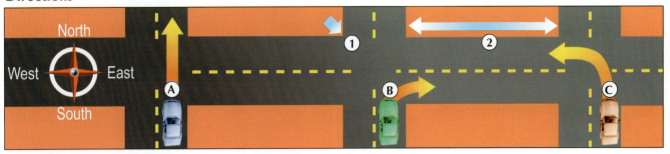

A. go straight

B. turn right

C. turn left

1. corner

2. block

Signs

3. stop

4. do not enter/wrong way

5. speed limit

6. one way

7. U-turn OK

8. no outlet/dead end

9. right turn only

10. pedestrian crossing

11. railroad crossing

12. no parking

13. school crossing

14. handicapped parking

More vocabulary

right-of-way: the right to go first

yield: to give another person or car the right-of-way

Share your answers.

1. Which traffic signs are the same in your country?

2. Do pedestrians have the right-of-way in your city?

3. What is the speed limit in front of your school? your home?

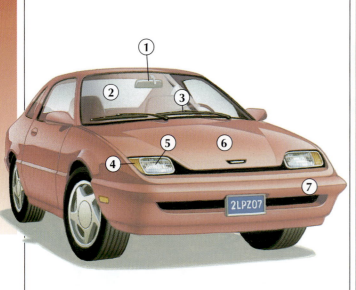

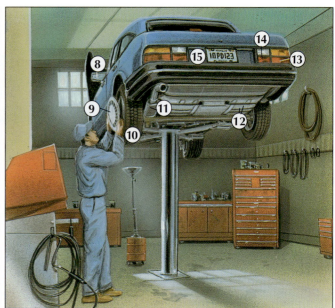

1. rearview mirror	**10.** tire	**19.** oil gauge	**28.** air conditioning
2. windshield	**11.** muffler	**20.** speedometer	**29.** heater
3. windshield wipers	**12.** gas tank	**21.** odometer	**30.** tape deck
4. turn signal	**13.** brake light	**22.** gas gauge	**31.** radio
5. headlight	**14.** taillight	**23.** temperature gauge	**32.** cigarette lighter
6. hood	**15.** license plate	**24.** horn	**33.** glove compartment
7. bumper	**16.** air bag	**25.** ignition	
8. sideview mirror	**17.** dashboard	**26.** steering wheel	
9. hubcap	**18.** turn signal	**27.** gearshift	

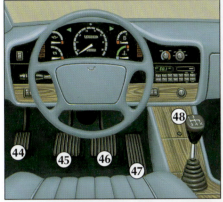
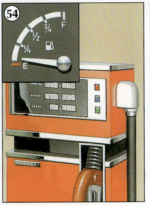

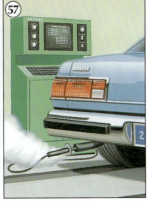

34. lock

35. front seat

36. seat belt

37. shoulder harness

38. backseat

39. child safety seat

40. fuel injection system

41. engine

42. radiator

43. battery

44. emergency brake

45. clutch*

46. brake pedal

47. accelerator/gas pedal

48. stick shift

49. trunk

50. lug wrench

51. jack

52. jumper cables

53. spare tire

54. The car needs **gas**.

55. The car needs **oil**.

56. The radiator needs **coolant**.

57. The car needs **a smog check**.

58. The battery needs **recharging**.

59. The tires need **air**.

*Note: Standard transmission cars have a clutch; automatic transmission cars do not.

1. airline terminal	**9.** airplane	**17.** baggage claim area
2. airline representative	**10.** overhead compartment	**18.** carousel
3. check-in counter	**11.** cockpit	**19.** luggage carrier
4. arrival and departure monitors	**12.** pilot	**20.** customs
5. gate	**13.** flight attendant	**21.** customs officer
6. boarding area	**14.** oxygen mask	**22.** declaration form
7. control tower	**15.** airsickness bag	**23.** passenger
8. helicopter	**16.** tray table	

A. **buy** your ticket

B. **check** your bags

C. **go through** security

D. **check in** at the gate

E. **get** your boarding pass

F. **board** the plane

G. **find** your seat

H. **stow** your carry-on bag

I. **fasten** your seat belt

J. **look for** the emergency exit

K. **look at** the emergency card

L. **take off / leave**

M. **request** a blanket

N. **experience** turbulence

O. **land / arrive**

P. **claim** your baggage

More vocabulary

destination: the place the passenger is going

departure time: the time the plane takes off

arrival time: the time the plane lands

direct flight: a plane trip between two cities with no stops

stopover: a stop before reaching the destination, sometimes to change planes

1. public school

2. private school

3. parochial school

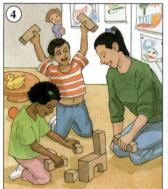

4. preschool

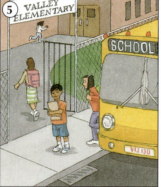

5. elementary school

6. middle school/
junior high school

7. high school

8. adult school

9. vocational school/trade school

10. college/university

Note: In the U.S. most children begin school at age 5 (in kindergarten) and graduate from high school at 17 or 18.

More vocabulary

When students graduate from a college or university they receive a **degree:**

Bachelor's degree — usually 4 years of study

Master's degree — an additional 1–3 years of study

Doctorate — an additional 3–5 years of study

community college: a two-year college where students can get an Associate of Arts degree.

graduate school: a school in a university where students study for their master's and doctorates.

1. writing assignment

A. Write a first draft.

B. Edit your paper.

C. Get feedback.

D. Rewrite your paper.

E. Turn in your paper.

2. paper/composition

My life in the U.S.

I arrived in this country in 1996. My family did not come with me. I was homesick, nervous, and a little excited. I had no job and no friends here. I lived with my aunt and my daily routine was always the same: get up, look for a job, go to bed. At night I remembered my mother's words to me, "Son, you can always come home!" I was homesick and scared, but I did not go home.

I started to study English at night. English is a difficult language and many times I was too tired to study. One teacher, Mrs. Armstrong, was very kind to me. She showed me many

3. title

4. sentence

5. paragraph

Punctuation

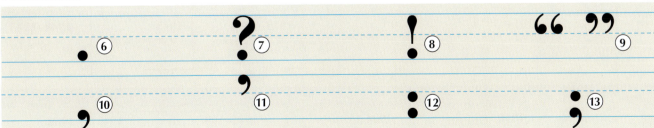

6. period

7. question mark

8. exclamation mark

9. quotation marks

10. comma

11. apostrophe

12. colon

13. semicolon

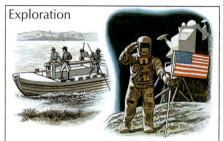

Exploration

War

Immigration

Historical and Political Events

1492 →
French, Spanish, English explorers

1607–1750
Colonies along Atlantic coast founded by Northern Europeans

1619 1st African slave sold in Virginia

1653 1st Indian reservation in Virginia

Before 1700   1700

Immigration*

1607
1st English in Virginia

1610
Spanish at Santa Fe

Population**   Before 1700: Native American: 1,000,000+   1700: colonists: 250,000

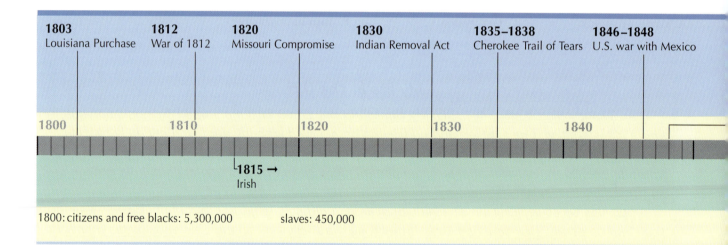

1803
Louisiana Purchase

1812
War of 1812

1820
Missouri Compromise

1830
Indian Removal Act

1835–1838
Cherokee Trail of Tears

1846–1848
U.S. war with Mexico

1800   1810   1820   1830   1840

1815 →
Irish

1800: citizens and free blacks: 5,300,000   slaves: 450,000

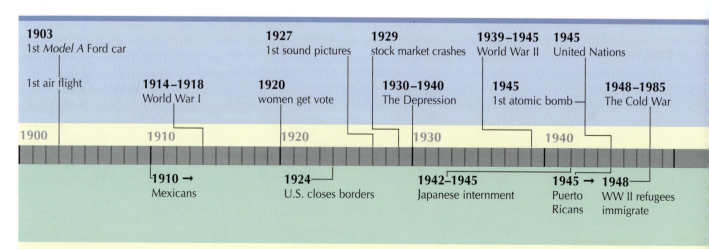

1903
1st *Model A* Ford car

1st air flight

1914–1918
World War I

1927
1st sound pictures

1920
women get vote

1929
stock market crashes

1930–1940
The Depression

1939–1945
World War II

1945
1st atomic bomb

1945 United Nations

1948–1985
The Cold War

1900   1910   1920   1930   1940

1910 →
Mexicans

1924—
U.S. closes borders

1942–1945
Japanese internment

1945 →
Puerto Ricans

1948—
WW II refugees immigrate

1900: 75,994,000

*Immigration dates indicate a time when large numbers of that group first began to immigrate to the U.S.
**All population figures before 1790 are estimates. Figures after 1790 are based on the official U.S. census.

Movement

Election

Invention

1754–1763
French and Indian War

1775–1783
Revolutionary War

1776
Declaration of
Independence

1788
U.S. Constitution

1791
Bill of Rights

1789 Washington 1st President

1750 1760 1770 1780 1790

1750 →
Scots, Irish, Germans

1790 →
Haitians

1750: Native American: 1,000,000 +   colonists and free blacks: 1,171,000   slaves: 200,000

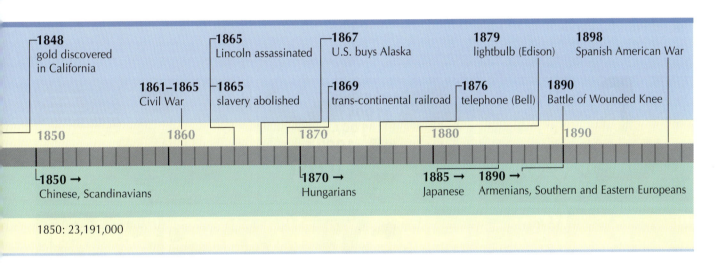

1848
gold discovered
in California

1865
Lincoln assassinated

1867
U.S. buys Alaska

1879
lightbulb (Edison)

1898
Spanish American War

1861–1865
Civil War

1865
slavery abolished

1869
trans-continental railroad

1876
telephone (Bell)

1890
Battle of Wounded Knee

1850 1860 1870 1880 1890

1850 →
Chinese, Scandinavians

1870 →
Hungarians

1885 →
Japanese

1890 →
Armenians, Southern and Eastern Europeans

1850: 23,191,000

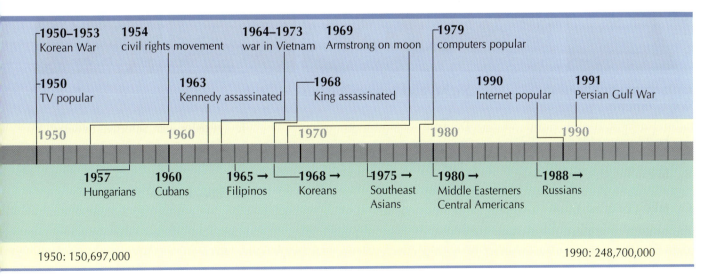

1950–1953
Korean War

1954
civil rights movement

1964–1973
war in Vietnam

1969
Armstrong on moon

1979
computers popular

1950
TV popular

1963
Kennedy assassinated

1968
King assassinated

1990
Internet popular

1991
Persian Gulf War

1950 1960 1970 1980 1990

1957
Hungarians

1960
Cubans

1965 →
Filipinos

1968 →
Koreans

1975 →
Southeast
Asians

1980 →
Middle Easterners
Central Americans

1988 →
Russians

1950: 150,697,000

1990: 248,700,000

BRANCHES OF GOVERNMENT

Legislative

Executive

Judicial

1. The House of Representatives

2. congresswoman/congressman

3. The Senate

4. senator

5. The White House

6. president

7. vice president

8. The Supreme Court

9. chief justice

10. justices

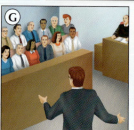

Citizenship application requirements

A. **be** 18 years old

B. **live** in the U.S. for five years

C. **take** a citizenship test

Rights and responsibilities

D. **vote**

E. **pay** taxes

F. **register** with Selective Service*

G. **serve** on a jury

H. **obey** the law

*Note: All males 18 to 26 who live in the U.S. are required to register with Selective Service.

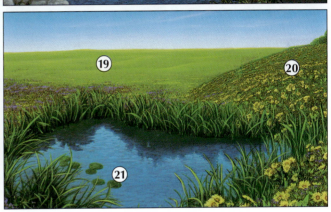

1. rain forest	**7.** peninsula	**13.** lake	**19.** plains
2. waterfall	**8.** island	**14.** mountain peak	**20.** meadow
3. river	**9.** bay	**15.** mountain range	**21.** pond
4. desert	**10.** beach	**16.** hills	
5. sand dune	**11.** forest	**17.** canyon	
6. ocean	**12.** shore	**18.** valley	

More vocabulary
a body of water: a river, lake, or ocean
stream/creek: a very small river

Talk about where you live and where you like to go.
I live in a valley. There is a lake nearby.
I like to go to the beach.

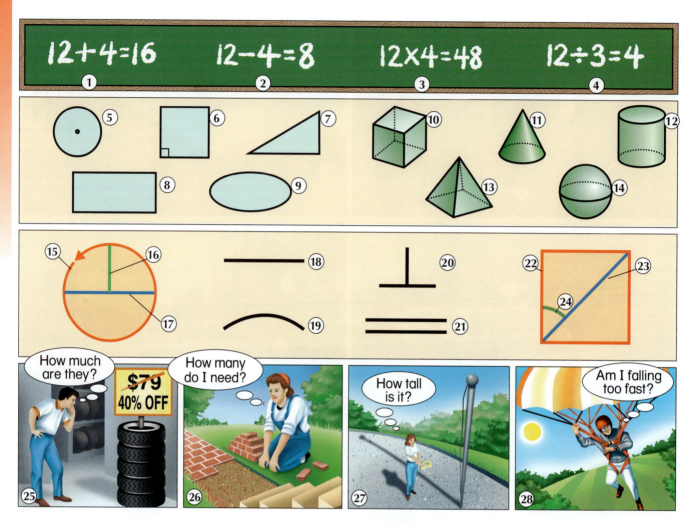

Operations

1. addition
2. subtraction
3. multiplication
4. division

Shapes

5. circle
6. square
7. triangle
8. rectangle
9. oval/ellipse

Solids

10. cube
11. cone
12. cylinder
13. pyramid
14. sphere

Parts of a circle

15. circumference
16. radius
17. diameter

Lines

18. straight
19. curved
20. perpendicular
21. parallel

Parts of a square

22. side
23. diagonal
24. angle

Types of math

25. algebra
26. geometry
27. trigonometry
28. calculus

More vocabulary

total: the answer to an addition problem
difference: the answer to a subtraction problem
product: the answer to a multiplication problem

quotient: the answer to a division problem
pi (π): the number when you divide the circumference of a circle by its diameter (approximately = 3.14)

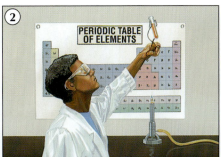

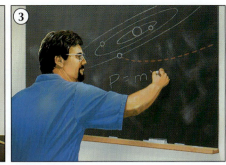

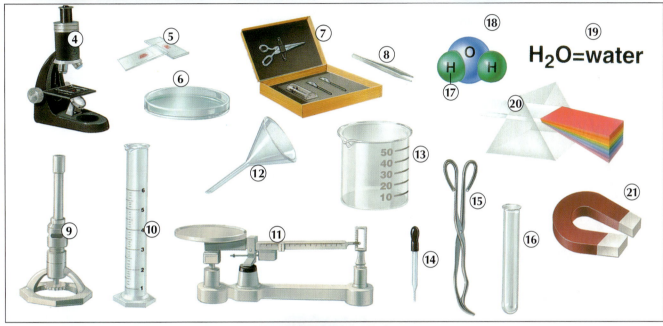

$H_2O = water$

1. biology

2. chemistry

3. physics

4. microscope

5. slide

6. petri dish

7. dissection kit

8. forceps

9. Bunsen burner

10. graduated cylinder

11. balance

12. funnel

13. beaker

14. dropper

15. crucible tongs

16. test tube

17. atom

18. molecule

19. formula

20. prism

21. magnet

A. **do** an experiment

B. **observe**

C. **record** results

A. **play** an instrument

B. **sing** a song

1. orchestra

2. rock band

Woodwinds

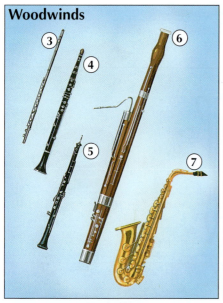

Strings

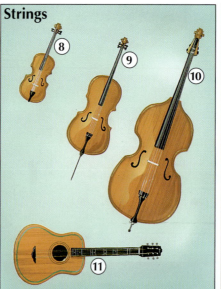

Brass

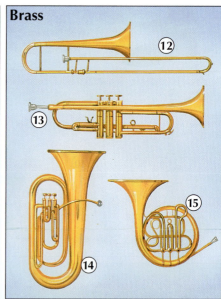

Percussion

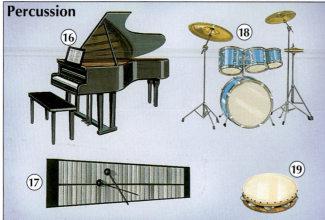

Other Instruments

3. flute	8. violin	13. trumpet/horn	18. drums
4. clarinet	9. cello	14. tuba	19. tambourine
5. oboe	10. bass	15. French horn	20. electric keyboard
6. bassoon	11. guitar	16. piano	21. accordion
7. saxophone	12. trombone	17. xylophone	22. organ

It's a chair.

C'est une chaise.

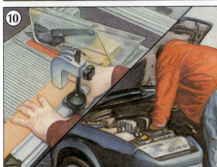

1. art

2. business education

3. chorus

4. computer science

5. driver's education

6. economics

7. English as a second language

8. foreign language

9. home economics

10. industrial arts/shop

11. PE (physical education)

12. theater arts

More vocabulary

core course: a subject students have to take

elective: a subject students choose to take

Share your answers.

1. What are your favorite subjects?

2. In your opinion, what subjects are most important? Why?

3. What foreign languages are taught in your school?

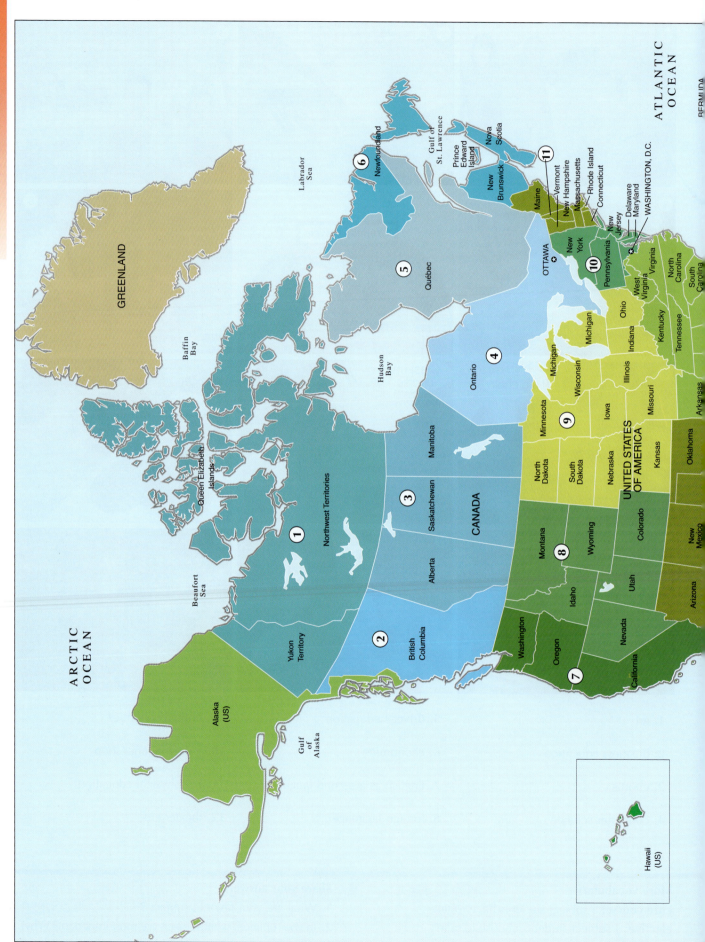

ATLANTIC OCEAN

BERMUDA

Labrador Sea

Gulf of St. Lawrence

Newfoundland

⑥

Prince Edward Island

Nova Scotia

New Brunswick

⑪

Maine

Vermont

New Hampshire

Massachusetts

Rhode Island

Connecticut

New Jersey

Delaware

Maryland

WASHINGTON, D.C.

New York

⑩

Pennsylvania

West Virginia

Virginia

North Carolina

South Carolina

GREENLAND

Baffin Bay

⑤

Québec

OTTAWA

Ohio

Kentucky

Tennessee

Michigan

Indiana

Michigan

Wisconsin

⑨

Illinois

Arkansas

Queen Elizabeth Islands

Hudson Bay

Ontario

④

Minnesota

Iowa

Missouri

Manitoba

North Dakota

South Dakota

Nebraska

Kansas

UNITED STATES OF AMERICA

Oklahoma

Northwest Territories

③

Saskatchewan

CANADA

Montana

⑧

Wyoming

Colorado

New Mexico

①

Alberta

Idaho

Utah

Arizona

Beaufort Sea

②

British Columbia

Washington

Nevada

Yukon Territory

ARCTIC OCEAN

⑦

Oregon

California

Alaska (US)

Gulf of Alaska

Hawaii (US)

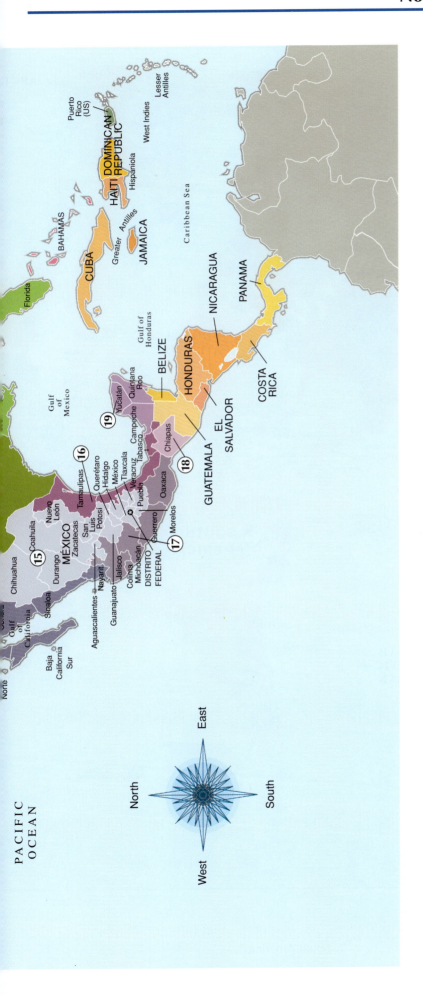

Regions of Mexico

14. The Pacific Northwest

15. The Plateau of Mexico

16. The Gulf Coastal Plain

17. The Southern Uplands

18. The Chiapas Highlands

19. The Yucatan Peninsula

Regions of the United States

7. The Pacific States/the West Coast

8. The Rocky Mountain States

9. The Midwest

10. The Mid-Atlantic States

11. New England

12. The Southwest

13. The Southeast/the South

Regions of Canada

1. Northern Canada

2. British Columbia

3. The Prairie Provinces

4. Ontario

5. Québec

6. The Atlantic Provinces

The World

Continents

1. North America   2. South America

CEAN

SVALBARD
(NORWAY)

FRANZ JOSEF LAND
(RUSSIA)

Barents Sea

RUSSIA

④ ASIA

③

KAZAKHSTAN

MONGOLIA

Caspian
Sea

Black Sea GEORGIA
AZERBAIJAN
ARMENIA

UZBEKISTAN KYRGYZSTAN

TURKEY TURKMENISTAN TAJIKISTAN

CYPRUS SYRIA
Mediterranean Sea LEBANON
ISRAEL IRAQ IRAN AFGHANISTAN

JORDAN KUWAIT

LIBYA EGYPT BAHRAIN
Persian
Gulf QATAR
SAUDI UNITED
ARABIA ARAB
EMIRATES

⑤

Red OMAN Arabian
Sea Sea

CHAD YEMEN

ERITREA

FRICA SUDAN DJIBOUTI SOMALIA

SOCOTRA
(YEMEN)

CENTRAL
AFRICAN
REPUBLIC ETHIOPIA

EROON

UGANDA KENYA

NGO
ON DEMOCRATIC RWANDA
REPUBLIC BURUNDI
OF THE
CONGO TANZANIA ZANZIBAR

ANGOLA ZAMBIA MALAWI

MOZAMBIQUE

ZIMBABWE

NAMIBIA BOTSWANA

SWAZILAND

LESOTHO

SOUTH
AFRICA

NORTH
KOREA Sea of
Japan
SOUTH
KOREA JAPAN

CHINA

East
China
Sea

NEPAL BHUTAN

INDIA BANGLADESH TAIWAN

MYANMAR
LAOS HONG
KONG

ANDAMAN THAILAND HAINAN
ISLANDS VIETNAM
(INDIA) CAMBODIA PHILIPPINES

NICOBAR South
ISLANDS China
(INDIA) Sea BRUNEI

MALDIVE SRI MALAYSIA
ISLANDS LANKA SINGAPORE
SUMATRA BORNEO CELEBES

CHAGOS ARCHIPELAGO

JAVA INDONESIA

SEYCHELLES

COMOROS

MADAGASCAR MAURITIUS

INDIAN
OCEAN

Bering
Sea

ALEUTIAN ISLANDS
(US)

Sea of
Okhotsk

NORTH
PACIFIC
OCEAN

VOLCANO
ISLANDS

DAITO
ISLANDS
(JAPAN)

PARECE
VELA
(JAPAN)

Philippine
Sea YAP
ISLANDS PALAU

WAKE ISLAND
(US)

NORTHERN
MARIANA
ISLANDS
(US)

GUAM
(US)

FEDERATED STATE
OF MICRONESIA

MARSHALL
ISLANDS

NAURU KIRIBATI

NEW GUINEA
PAPUA
NEW
GUINEA SOLOMON
ISLANDS

TUVALU

Coral
Sea VANUATU FIJI

CORAL SEA
ISLANDS
TERRITORY
(AUSTRALIA) NEW
CALEDONIA

⑥ AUSTRALIA

TASMANIA
(AUSTRALIA)

NORTH
ISLAND
NEW
ZEALAND
SOUTH
ISLAND

SOUTH
PACIFIC
OCEAN

OUTHERN
OCEAN

ICELAND

NORWAY FINLAND

SWEDEN

North
Sea Baltic
Sea ESTONIA RUSSIA

DENMARK LATVIA
NETHER- LITHUANIA
LANDS RUSSIA

IRELAND UNITED
KINGDOM GERMANY BELARUS

BELGIUM POLAND
LUXEMBOURG CZECH
LIECHTENSTEIN REPUBLIC SLOVAKIA UKRAINE

SWITZER- AUSTRIA MOLDOVA
LAND SLOVENIA HUNGARY
FRANCE CROATIA ROMANIA
BOSNIA- SERBIA
ANDORRA CORSICA HERZEGOVINA
(FR) MONTENEGRO BULGARIA Black Sea
SPAIN MONACO ITALY MACEDONIA
SARDINIA ALBANIA
PORTUGAL BALEARIC (IT) GREECE
ISLANDS
(SP) SICILY (IT)

MALTA CRETE CYPRUS

Mediterranean Sea

ANTARCTICA ⑦

Energy and the Environment

Energy resources

1. solar energy

2. wind

3. natural gas

4. coal

5. hydroelectric power

6. oil/petroleum

7. geothermal energy

8. nuclear energy

Pollution

9. hazardous waste

10. air pollution/smog

11. acid rain

12. water pollution

13. radiation

14. pesticide poisoning

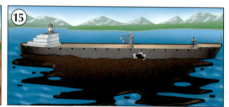

15. oil spill

Conservation

A. **recycle**

B. **save** water/**conserve** water

C. **save** energy/**conserve** energy

Share your answers.

1. How do you heat your home?

2. Do you have a gas stove or an electric stove?

3. What are some ways you can save energy when it's cold?

4. Do you recycle? What products do you recycle?

5. Does your market have recycling bins?

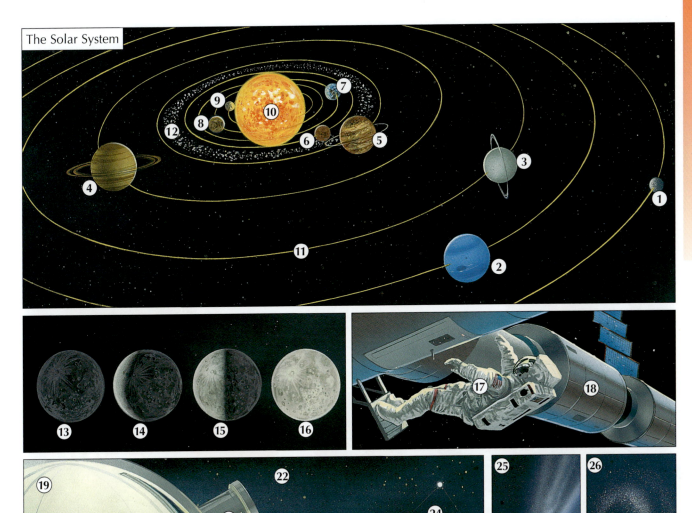

The Solar System

The planets

1. Pluto

2. Neptune

3. Uranus

4. Saturn

5. Jupiter

6. Mars

7. Earth

8. Venus

9. Mercury

10. sun

11. orbit

12. asteroid belt

13. new moon

14. crescent moon

15. quarter moon

16. full moon

17. astronaut

18. space station

19. observatory

20. astronomer

21. telescope

22. space

23. star

24. constellation

25. comet

26. galaxy

More vocabulary

lunar eclipse: when the earth is between the sun and the moon

solar eclipse: when the moon is between the earth and the sun

Share your answers.

1. Do you know the names of any constellations?

2. How do you feel when you look up at the night sky?

3. Is the night sky in the U.S. the same as in your country?

Trees and Plants

Parts of a tree

1. twig
2. branch
3. limb
4. trunk
5. root
6. leaf

7. redwood	**10.** pine	**13.** maple	**16.** dogwood
8. birch	**11.** pinecone	**14.** willow	**17.** elm
9. magnolia	**12.** needle	**15.** palm	**18.** oak

Plants

19. holly	**21.** cactus	**23.** poison oak	**25.** poison ivy
20. berries	**22.** vine	**24.** poison sumac	

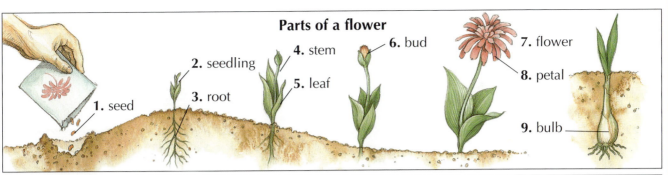

Parts of a flower

1. seed
2. seedling
3. root
4. stem
5. leaf
6. bud
7. flower
8. petal
9. bulb

10. sunflower	15. rose	20. iris	25. crocus
11. tulip	16. gardenia	21. jasmine	26. daffodil
12. hibiscus	17. orchid	22. violet	27. bouquet
13. marigold	18. carnation	23. poinsettia	28. thorn
14. daisy	19. chrysanthemum	24. lily	29. houseplant

Marine Life, Amphibians, and Reptiles

Parts of a fish

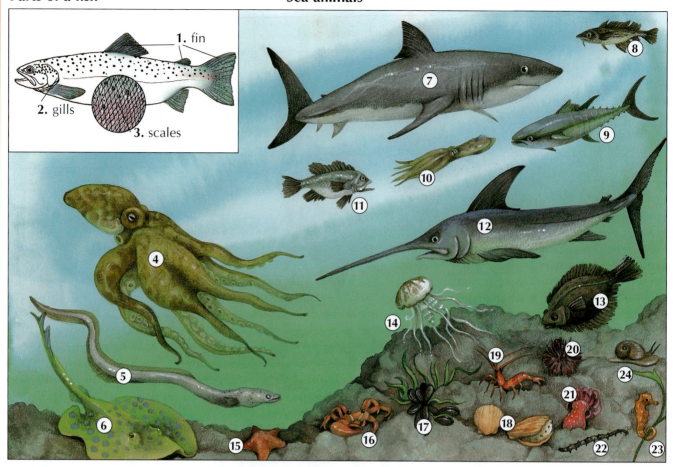

1. fin
2. gills
3. scales

Sea animals

4. octopus	**11.** bass	**18.** scallop
5. eel	**12.** swordfish	**19.** shrimp
6. ray	**13.** flounder	**20.** sea urchin
7. shark	**14.** jellyfish	**21.** sea anemone
8. cod	**15.** starfish	**22.** worm
9. tuna	**16.** crab	**23.** sea horse
10. squid	**17.** mussel	**24.** snail

Amphibians

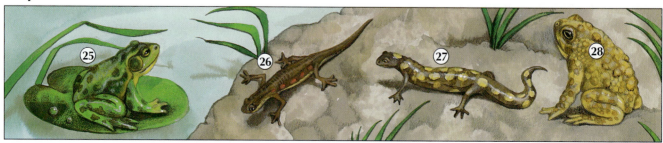

25. frog   **26.** newt   **27.** salamander   **28.** toad

Sea mammals

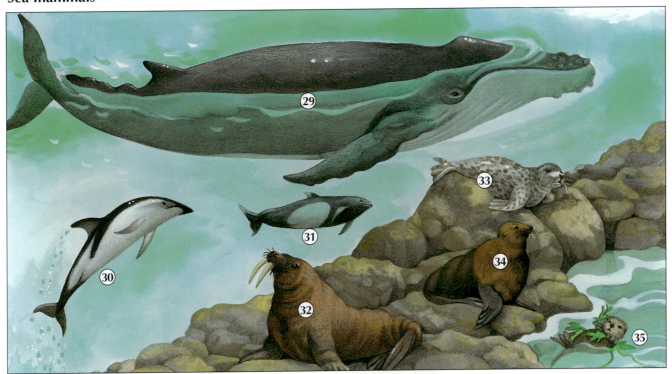

29. whale

30. dolphin

31. porpoise

32. walrus

33. seal

34. sea lion

35. otter

Reptiles

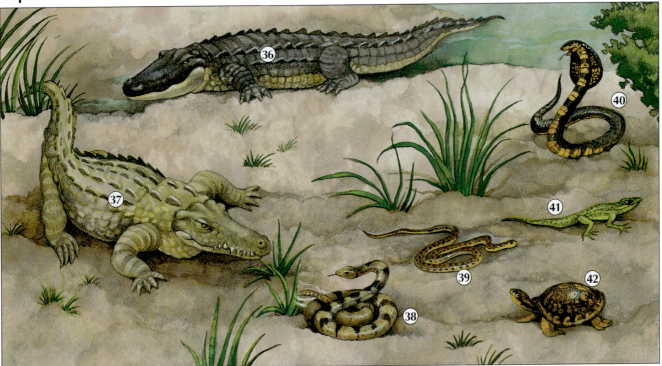

36. alligator

37. crocodile

38. rattlesnake

39. garter snake

40. cobra

41. lizard

42. turtle

Birds, Insects, and Arachnids

Parts of a bird

1. beak/bill
2. wing
3. nest
4. claw
5. feather

6. owl
7. blue jay
8. sparrow
9. woodpecker
10. eagle
11. hummingbird
12. penguin
13. duck
14. goose
15. peacock
16. pigeon
17. robin

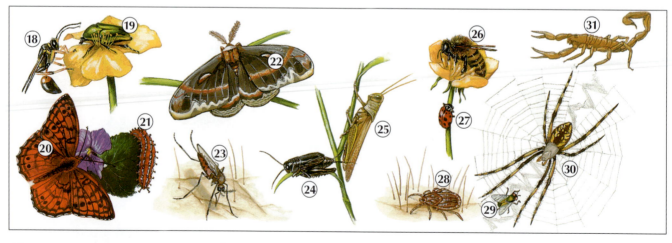

18. wasp
19. beetle
20. butterfly
21. caterpillar
22. moth
23. mosquito
24. cricket
25. grasshopper
26. honeybee
27. ladybug
28. tick
29. fly
30. spider
31. scorpion

Farm animals

1. goat

2. donkey

3. cow

4. horse

5. hen

6. rooster

7. sheep

8. pig

Pets

9. cat

10. kitten

11. dog

12. puppy

13. rabbit

14. guinea pig

15. parakeet

16. goldfish

Rodents

17. mouse

18. rat

19. gopher

20. chipmunk

21. squirrel

22. prairie dog

More vocabulary

Wild animals live, eat, and raise their young away from people, in the forests, mountains, plains, etc.

Domesticated animals work for people or live with them.

Share your answers.

1. Do you have any pets? any farm animals?
2. Which of these animals are in your neighborhood? Which are not?

1. moose	5. wolf	9. beaver	13. raccoon
2. mountain lion	6. buffalo/bison	10. porcupine	14. deer
3. coyote	7. bat	11. bear	15. fox
4. opossum	8. armadillo	12. skunk	

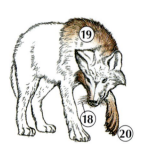

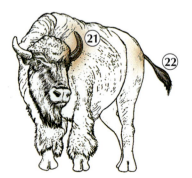

16. antler	18. whiskers	20. paw	22. tail
17. hoof	19. coat/fur	21. horn	23. quill

24. anteater	**30.** gorilla	**36.** lion	**42.** elephant
25. leopard	**31.** hyena	**37.** tiger	**43.** hippopotamus
26. llama	**32.** baboon	**38.** camel	**44.** kangaroo
27. monkey	**33.** giraffe	**39.** panther	**45.** koala
28. chimpanzee	**34.** zebra	**40.** orangutan	**46.** platypus
29. rhinoceros	**35.** antelope	**41.** panda	

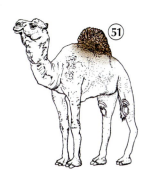

47. trunk   **48.** tusk   **49.** mane   **50.** pouch   **51.** hump

1. accountant

2. actor

3. administrative assistant

4. architect

5. artist

6. assembler

7. auto mechanic

8. baker

9. bricklayer

10. businessman / businesswoman

11. butcher

12. caregiver / baby-sitter

13. carpenter

14. cashier

15. commercial fisher

16. computer programmer

Use the new language.

1. Who works outside?

2. Who works inside?

3. Who makes things?

4. Who uses a computer?

5. Who wears a uniform?

6. Who sells things?

17. cook

18. delivery person

19. dental assistant

20. dentist

21. dockworker

22. doctor

23. engineer

24. firefighter

25. florist

26. gardener

27. garment worker

28. gas station attendant

29. graphic artist

30. hairdresser

31. home attendant

32. homemaker

Share your answers.

1. Do you know people who have some of these jobs? What do they say about their work?

2. Which of these jobs are available in your city?

3. For which of these jobs do you need special training?

33. housekeeper	**39.** model	**45.** postal worker
34. interpreter / translator	**40.** mover	**46.** printer
35. janitor / custodian	**41.** musician	**47.** receptionist
36. lawyer	**42.** nurse	**48.** repair person
37. machine operator	**43.** painter	
38. messenger / courier	**44.** police officer	

Talk about each of the jobs or occupations.

She's a housekeeper. She works in a hotel.
He's an interpreter. He works for the government.

She's a nurse. She works with patients.

49. reporter

50. salesclerk / salesperson

51. sanitation worker

52. secretary

53. server

54. serviceman / servicewoman

55. stock clerk

56. store owner

57. student

58. teacher / instructor

59. telemarketer

60. travel agent

61. truck driver

62. veterinarian

63. welder

64. writer / author

Talk about your job or the job you want.

What do you do?

  I'm <u>a salesclerk.</u> I work in <u>a store.</u>

What do you want to do?

  I want to be <u>a veterinarian</u>. I want to work with <u>animals</u>.

Job Skills

A. **assemble** components

B. **assist** medical patients

C. **cook**

D. **do** manual labor

E. **drive** a truck

F. **operate** heavy machinery

G. **repair** appliances

H. **sell** cars

I. **sew** clothes

J. **speak** another language

K. **supervise** people

L. **take care** of children

M. **type**

N. **use** a cash register

O. **wait on** customers

P. **work** on a computer

More vocabulary

act: to perform in a play, movie, or TV show

fly: to pilot an airplane

teach: to instruct, to show how to do something

Share your answers.

1. What job skills do you have? Where did you learn them?

2. What job skills do you want to learn?

A. talk to friends

B. look at a job board

C. look for a help wanted sign

D. look in the classifieds

E. call for information

F. ask about the hours

G. fill out an application

H. go on an interview

I. talk about your experience

J. ask about benefits

K. inquire about the salary

L. get hired

An Office

1. desk

2. typewriter

3. secretary

4. microcassette transcriber

5. stacking tray

6. desk calendar

7. desk pad

8. calculator

9. electric pencil sharpener

10. file cabinet

11. file folder

12. file clerk

13. supply cabinet

14. photocopier

A. **take** a message

B. **fax** a letter

C. **transcribe** notes

D. **type** a letter

E. **make** copies

F. **collate** papers

G. **staple**

H. **file** papers

Practice taking messages.

Hello. My name is Sara Scott. Is Mr. Lee in?

Not yet. Would you like to leave a message?

Yes. Please ask him to call me at 555-4859.

Share your answers.

1. Which office equipment do you know how to use?

2. Which jobs does a file clerk do?

3. Which jobs does a secretary do?

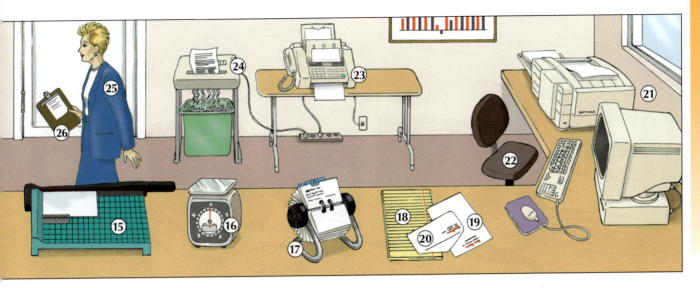

15. paper cutter

16. postal scale

17. rotary card file

18. legal pad

19. letterhead paper

20. envelope

21. computer workstation

22. swivel chair

23. fax machine

24. paper shredder

25. office manager

26. clipboard

27. appointment book

28. stapler

29. staple

30. organizer

31. typewriter cartridge

32. mailer

33. correction fluid

34. Post-it notes

35. label

36. notepad

37. glue

38. rubber cement

39. clear tape

40. rubber stamp

41. ink pad

42. packing tape

43. pushpin

44. paper clip

45. rubber band

Use the new language.

1. Which items keep things together?

2. Which items are used to mail packages?

3. Which items are made of paper?

Share your answers.

1. Which office supplies do students use?

2. Where can you buy them?

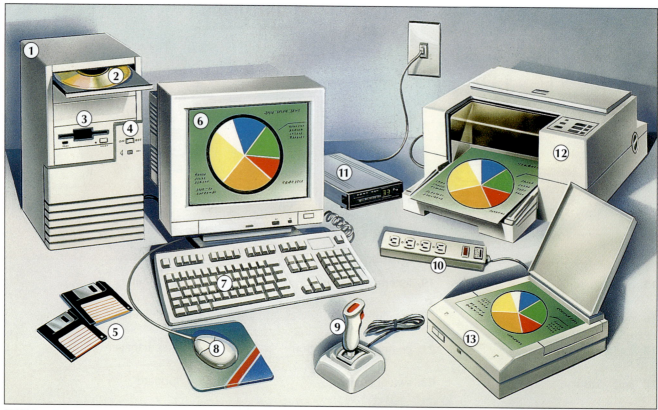

Hardware

1. CPU (central processing unit)

2. CD-ROM disc

3. disk drive

4. power switch

5. disk/floppy

6. monitor/screen

7. keyboard

8. mouse

9. joystick

10. surge protector

11. modem

12. printer

13. scanner

14. laptop

15. trackball

16. cable

17. port

18. motherboard

19. slot

20. hard disk drive

Software

21. program/application

22. user's manual

More vocabulary

data: information that a computer can read

memory: how much data a computer can hold

speed: how fast a computer can work with data

Share your answers.

1. Can you use a computer?

2. How did you learn? in school? from a book? by yourself?

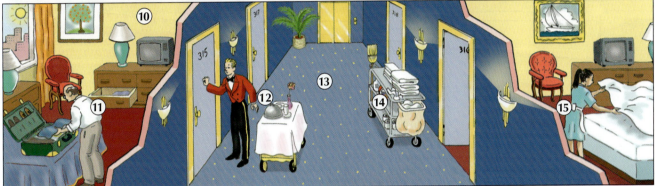

1. valet parking	**8.** front desk	**15.** housekeeper
2. doorman	**9.** desk clerk	**16.** pool
3. lobby	**10.** guest room	**17.** pool service
4. bell captain	**11.** guest	**18.** ice machine
5. bellhop	**12.** room service	**19.** meeting room
6. luggage cart	**13.** hall	**20.** ballroom
7. gift shop	**14.** housekeeping cart	

More vocabulary

concierge: the hotel worker who helps guests find restaurants and interesting places to go

service elevator: an elevator for hotel workers

Share your answers.

1. Does this look like a hotel in your city? Which one?
2. Which hotel job is the most difficult?
3. How much does it cost to stay in a hotel in your city?

1. front office	7. parts	13. packer
2. factory owner	8. assembly line	14. forklift
3. designer	9. warehouse	15. shipping clerk
4. time clock	10. order puller	16. loading dock
5. line supervisor	11. hand truck	
6. factory worker	12. conveyor belt	

A. design

B. manufacture

C. ship

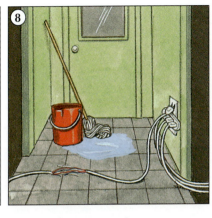

1. electrical hazard

2. flammable

3. poison

4. corrosive

5. biohazard

6. radioactive

7. hazardous materials

8. dangerous situation

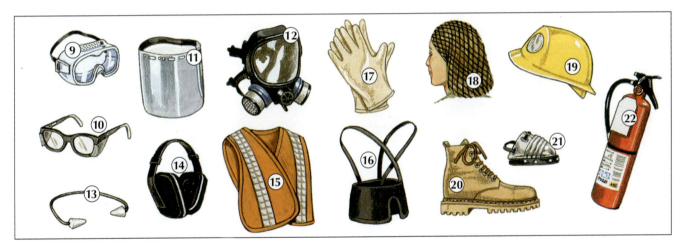

9. safety goggles

10. safety glasses

11. safety visor

12. respirator

13. earplugs

14. safety earmuffs

15. safety vest

16. back support

17. latex gloves

18. hair net

19. hard hat

20. safety boot

21. toe guard

22. fire extinguisher

23. careless

24. careful

Farming and Ranching

Crops

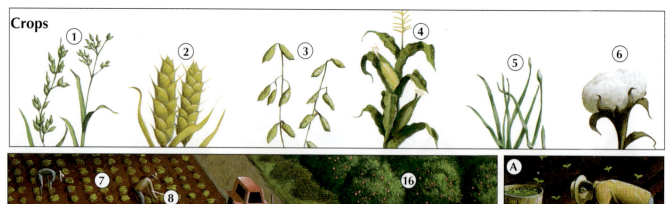

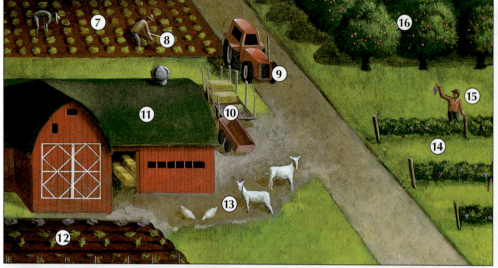

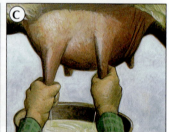

1. rice	**8.** farmworker	**15.** farmer / grower	**22.** rancher
2. wheat	**9.** tractor	**16.** orchard	**A. plant**
3. soybeans	**10.** farm equipment	**17.** corral	**B. harvest**
4. corn	**11.** barn	**18.** hay	**C. milk**
5. alfalfa	**12.** vegetable garden	**19.** fence	**D. feed**
6. cotton	**13.** livestock	**20.** hired hand	
7. field	**14.** vineyard	**21.** steers / cattle	

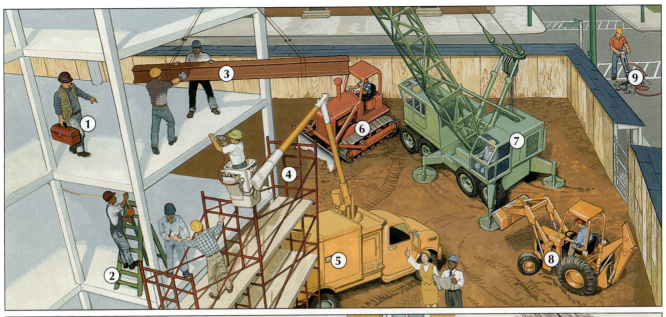

1. construction worker
2. ladder
3. I beam / girder
4. scaffolding
5. cherry picker
6. bulldozer
7. crane
8. backhoe
9. jackhammer / pneumatic drill

10. concrete
11. bricks
12. trowel
13. insulation
14. stucco
15. window pane
16. plywood
17. wood / lumber
18. drywall

19. shingles
20. pickax
21. shovel
22. sledgehammer

A. **paint**
B. **lay** bricks
C. **measure**
D. **hammer**

1. hammer
2. mallet
3. ax

4. handsaw
5. hacksaw
6. C-clamp

7. pliers
8. electric drill
9. power sander

10. circular saw
11. blade
12. router

21. vise
22. tape measure
23. drill bit
24. level

25. screwdriver
26. Phillips screwdriver
27. machine screw
28. wood screw

29. nail
30. bolt
31. nut
32. washer

33. toggle bolt
34. hook
35. eye hook
36. chain

Use the new language.
1. Which tools are used for plumbing?
2. Which tools are used for painting?

3. Which tools are used for electrical work?
4. Which tools are used for working with wood?

13. wire

14. extension cord

15. yardstick

16. pipe

17. fittings

18. wood

19. spray gun

20. paint

37. wire stripper

38. electrical tape

39. flashlight

40. battery

41. outlet

42. pipe wrench

43. wrench

44. plunger

45. paint pan

46. paint roller

47. paintbrush

48. scraper

49. masking tape

50. sandpaper

51. chisel

52. plane

Use the new language.

Look at **Household Problems and Repairs,**
pages **48–49.**

Name the tools you use to fix the problems you see.

Share your answers.

1. Which tools do you have in your home?

2. Which tools can be dangerous to use?

Places to Go

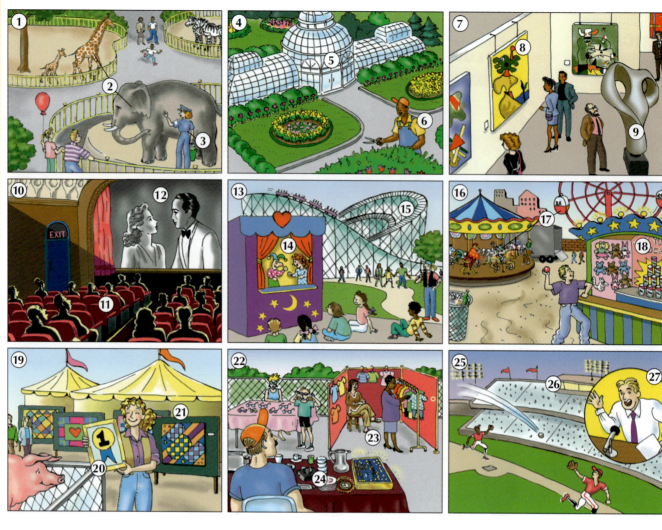

1. zoo

2. animals

3. zookeeper

4. botanical gardens

5. greenhouse

6. gardener

7. art museum

8. painting

9. sculpture

10. the movies

11. seat

12. screen

13. amusement park

14. puppet show

15. roller coaster

16. carnival

17. rides

18. game

19. county fair

20. first place/first prize

21. exhibition

22. swap meet/flea market

23. booth

24. merchandise

25. baseball game

26. stadium

27. announcer

Talk about the places you like to go.

I like _animals_, so I go to _the zoo_.

I like _rides_, so I go to _carnivals_.

Share your answers.

1. Which of these places is interesting to you?

2. Which rides do you like at an amusement park?

3. What are some famous places to go to in your country?

1. ball field

2. bike path

3. cyclist

4. bicycle/bike

5. jump rope

6. duck pond

7. tennis court

8. picnic table

9. tricycle

10. bench

11. water fountain

12. swings

13. slide

14. climbing apparatus

15. sandbox

16. seesaw

A. **pull** the wagon

B. **push** the swing

C. **climb** on the bars

D. **picnic/have** a picnic

1. camping

2. boating

3. canoeing

4. rafting

5. fishing

6. hiking

7. backpacking

8. mountain biking

9. horseback riding

10. tent

11. campfire

12. sleeping bag

13. foam pad

14. life vest

15. backpack

16. camping stove

17. fishing net

18. fishing pole

19. rope

20. multi-use knife

21. matches

22. lantern

23. insect repellent

24. canteen

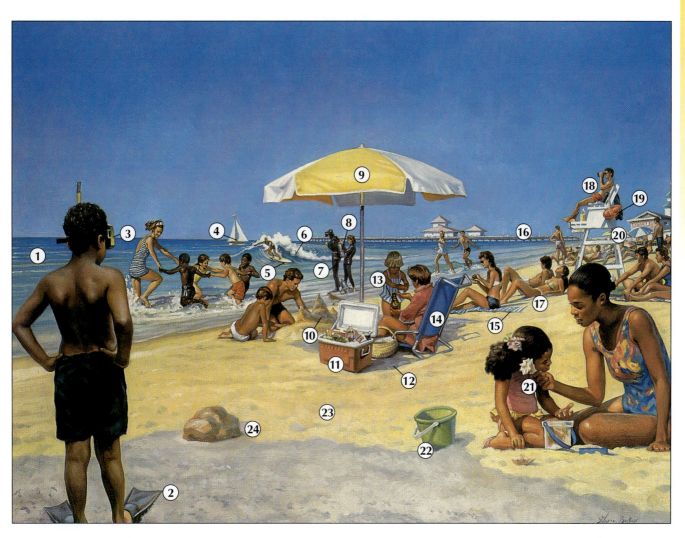

1. ocean/water

2. fins

3. diving mask

4. sailboat

5. surfboard

6. wave

7. wet suit

8. scuba tank

9. beach umbrella

10. sand castle

11. cooler

12. shade

13. sunscreen/sunblock

14. beach chair

15. beach towel

16. pier

17. sunbather

18. lifeguard

19. lifesaving device

20. lifeguard station

21. seashell

22. pail/bucket

23. sand

24. rock

More vocabulary

seaweed: a plant that grows in the ocean

tide: the level of the ocean. The tide goes in and out every twelve hours.

Share your answers.

1. Are there any beaches near your home?

2. Do you prefer to spend more time on the sand or in the water?

3. Where are some of the world's best beaches?

155

A. walk	E. catch	I. shoot	M. tackle
B. jog	F. pitch	J. jump	
C. run	G. hit	K. dribble / bounce	
D. throw	H. pass	L. kick	

Practice talking about what you can do.

I can swim, but I can't dive.

I can pass the ball well, but I can't shoot too well.

Use the new language.

Look at **Individual Sports,** page **159.**

Name the actions you see people doing.

The man in number 18 is riding a horse.

N. serve

O. swing

P. exercise / work out

Q. stretch

R. bend

S. dive

T. swim

U. ski

V. skate

W. ride

X. start

Y. race

Z. finish

Share your answers.

1. What do you like to do?
2. What do you have difficulty doing?

3. How often do you exercise? Once a week? Two or three times a week? More? Never?
4. Which is more difficult, throwing a ball or catching it?

1. score
2. coach
3. team
4. fan
5. player
6. official/referee
7. basketball court

8. basketball
9. baseball
10. softball
11. football
12. soccer
13. ice hockey
14. volleyball
15. water polo

More vocabulary

captain: the team leader
umpire: in baseball, the name for the referee
Little League: a baseball league for children

win: to have the best score
lose: the opposite of win
tie: to have the same score as the other team

1. archery

2. billiards/pool

3. bowling

4. cycling/biking

5. fencing

6. flying disc*

7. golf

8. gymnastics

9. inline skating

10. martial arts

11. racquetball

12. skateboarding

13. table tennis/
   Ping-Pong™

14. tennis

15. weightlifting

16. wrestling

17. track and field

18. horse racing

*Note: one brand is Frisbee®
(Mattel, Inc.)

Talk about sports.

Which sports do you like?

   I like tennis but I don't like golf.

Share your answers.

1. Which sports are good for children to learn? Why?

2. Which sport is the most difficult to learn? Why?

3. Which sport is the most dangerous? Why?

Winter Sports and Water Sports

1. downhill skiing

2. snowboarding

3. cross-country skiing

4. ice skating

5. figure skating

6. sledding

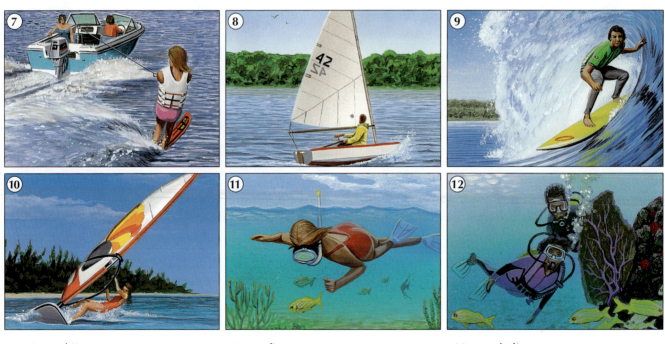

7. waterskiing

8. sailing

9. surfing

10. sailboarding

11. snorkeling

12. scuba diving

Use the new language.
Look at **The Beach,** page **155.**
Name the sports you see.

Share your answers.
1. Which sports are in the Winter Olympics?
2. Which sports do you think are the most exciting
   to watch?

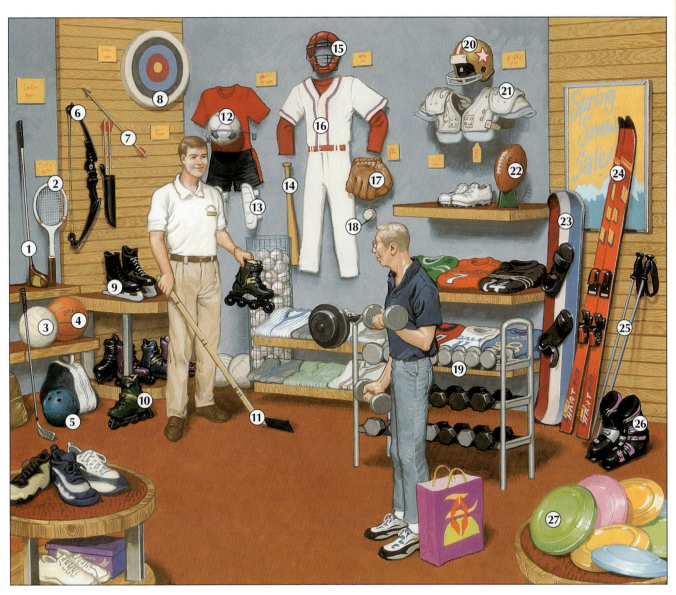

1. golf club	**8.** target	**15.** catcher's mask	**22.** football
2. tennis racket	**9.** ice skates	**16.** uniform	**23.** snowboard
3. volleyball	**10.** inline skates	**17.** glove	**24.** skis
4. basketball	**11.** hockey stick	**18.** baseball	**25.** ski poles
5. bowling ball	**12.** soccer ball	**19.** weights	**26.** ski boots
6. bow	**13.** shin guards	**20.** football helmet	**27.** flying disc*
7. arrow	**14.** baseball bat	**21.** shoulder pads	*Note: one brand is Frisbee® (Mattel, Inc.)

Share your answers.

1. Which sports equipment is used for safety reasons?
2. Which sports equipment is heavy?
3. What sports equipment do you have at home?

Use the new language.

Look at **Individual Sports**, page **159**.

Name the sports equipment you see.

A. collect things   **B. play** games   **C. build** models   **D. do** crafts

1. video game system

2. cartridge

3. board game

4. dice

5. checkers

6. chess

7. model kit

8. glue

9. acrylic paint

10. figurine

11. baseball card

12. stamp collection

13. coin collection

14. clay

15. doll making kit

16. woodworking kit

Talk about how much time you spend on your hobbies.

I *do crafts* all the time.

I *play chess* sometimes.

I never *build models*.

Share your answers.

1. How often do you play video games? Often? Sometimes? Never?

2. What board games do you know?

3. Do you collect anything? What?

E. paint　　　　**F. knit**　　　　**G. pretend**　　　　**H. play** cards

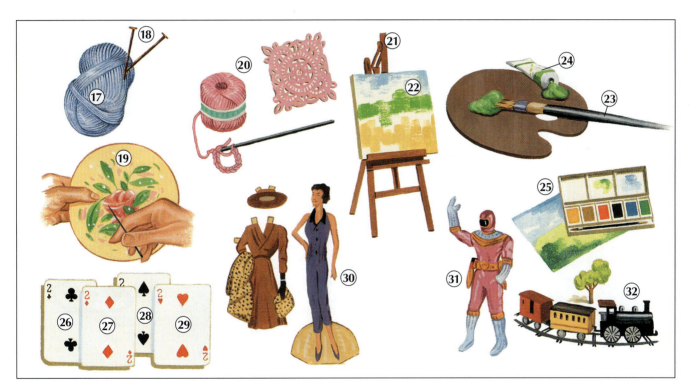

17. yarn	**21.** easel	**25.** watercolor	**29.** hearts
18. knitting needles	**22.** canvas	**26.** clubs	**30.** paper doll
19. embroidery	**23.** paintbrush	**27.** diamonds	**31.** action figure
20. crochet	**24.** oil paint	**28.** spades	**32.** model trains

Share your answers.

1. Do you like to play cards? Which games?

2. Did you pretend a lot when you were a child? What did you pretend to be?

3. Is it important to have hobbies? Why or why not?

4. What's your favorite game?

5. What's your hobby?

1. clock radio

2. portable radio-cassette player

3. cassette recorder

4. microphone

5. shortwave radio

6. TV (television)

7. portable TV

8. VCR (videocassette recorder)

9. remote control

10. videocassette

11. speakers

12. turntable

13. tuner

14. CD player

15. personal radio-cassette player

16. headphones

17. adapter

18. plug

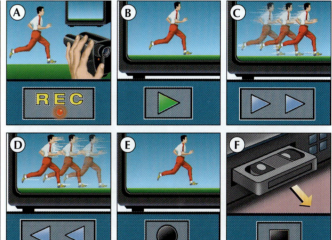

19. video camera	**27.** camera case	**35.** underexposed
20. tripod	**28.** screen	**A.** **record**
21. camcorder	**29.** carousel slide projector	**B.** **play**
22. battery pack	**30.** slide tray	**C.** **fast forward**
23. battery charger	**31.** slides	**D.** **rewind**
24. 35 mm camera	**32.** photo album	**E.** **pause**
25. zoom lens	**33.** out of focus	**F.** **stop** and **eject**
26. film	**34.** overexposed	

Entertainment

Types of entertainment

1. film/movie

2. play

3. television program

4. radio program

5. stand-up comedy

6. concert

7. ballet

8. opera

Types of stories

9. western

10. comedy

11. tragedy

12. science fiction story

13. action story/
adventure story

14. horror story

15. mystery

16. romance

166

Types of TV programs

17. news

18. sitcom (situation comedy)

19. cartoon

20. talk show

21. soap opera

22. nature program

23. game show / quiz show

24. children's program

25. shopping program

26. serious book

27. funny book

28. sad book

29. boring book

30. interesting book

① JAN **1** ②③

④ FEB **14** ⑤⑥

⑦ JULY **4** ⑧⑨

⑩ OCT **31** ⑪⑫⑬⑭

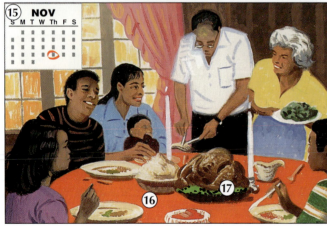
⑮ NOV ⑯⑰

⑱ DEC **25** ⑲⑳

1. New Year's Day
2. parade
3. confetti
4. Valentine's Day
5. card
6. heart
7. Independence Day/4th of July

8. fireworks
9. flag
10. Halloween
11. jack-o'-lantern
12. mask
13. costume
14. candy

15. Thanksgiving
16. feast
17. turkey
18. Christmas
19. ornament
20. Christmas tree

A. plan a party

B. invite the guests

C. decorate the house

D. wrap a gift

E. hide

F. answer the door

G. shout "surprise!"

H. light the candles

I. sing "Happy Birthday"

J. make a wish

K. blow out the candles

L. open the presents

Practice inviting friends to a party.

I'd love for you to come to my party <u>next week</u>.
Could <u>you and your friend</u> come to my party?
Would <u>your friend</u> like to come to a party I'm giving?

Share your answers.

1. Do you celebrate birthdays? What do you do?
2. Are there birthdays you celebrate in a special way?
3. Is there a special birthday song in your country?

Verb Guide

Verbs in English are either regular or irregular in the past tense and past participle forms.

Regular Verbs

The regular verbs below are marked 1, 2, 3, or 4 according to four different spelling patterns. (See page 172 for the **irregular verbs** which do not follow any of these patterns.)

Spelling Patterns for the Past and the Past Participle	*Example*		
1. Add **-ed** to the end of the verb.	ASK	→	ASKED
2. Add **-d** to the end of the verb.	LIVE	→	LIVED
3. Double the final consonant and add **-ed** to the end of the verb.	DROP	→	DROPPED
4. Drop the final y and add **-ied** to the end of the verb.	CRY	→	CRIED

The Oxford Picture Dictionary List of Regular Verbs

act (1)	collect (1)	exercise (2)
add (1)	color (1)	experience (2)
address (1)	comb (1)	exterminate (2)
answer (1)	commit (3)	fasten (1)
apologize (2)	compliment (1)	fax (1)
appear (1)	conserve (2)	file (2)
applaud (1)	convert (1)	fill (1)
arrange (2)	cook (1)	finish (1)
arrest (1)	copy (4)	fix (1)
arrive (2)	correct (1)	floss (1)
ask (1)	cough (1)	fold (1)
assemble (2)	count (1)	fry (4)
assist (1)	cross (1)	gargle (2)
bake (2)	cry (4)	graduate (2)
barbecue (2)	dance (2)	grate (2)
bathe (2)	design (1)	grease (2)
board (1)	deposit (1)	greet (1)
boil (1)	deliver (1)	grill (1)
borrow (1)	dial (1)	hail (1)
bounce (2)	dictate (2)	hammer (1)
brainstorm (1)	die (2)	harvest (1)
breathe (2)	discuss (1)	help (1)
broil (1)	dive (2)	hire (2)
brush (1)	dress (1)	hug (3)
burn (1)	dribble (2)	immigrate (2)
call (1)	drill (1)	inquire (2)
carry (4)	drop (3)	insert (1)
change (2)	drown (1)	introduce (2)
check (1)	dry (4)	invite (2)
choke (2)	dust (1)	iron (1)
chop (3)	dye (2)	jog (3)
circle (2)	edit (1)	join (1)
claim (1)	eject (1)	jump (1)
clap (3)	empty (4)	kick (1)
clean (1)	end (1)	kiss (1)
clear (1)	enter (1)	knit (3)
climb (1)	erase (2)	land (1)
close (2)	examine (2)	laugh (1)
collate (2)	exchange (2)	learn (1)

lengthen (1)
listen (1)
live (2)
load (1)
lock (1)
look (1)
mail (1)
manufacture (2)
mark (1)
match (1)
measure (2)
milk (1)
miss (1)
mix (1)
mop (3)
move (2)
mow (1)
need (1)
nurse (2)
obey (1)
observe (2)
open (1)
operate (2)
order (1)
overdose (2)
paint (1)
park (1)
pass (1)
pause (2)
peel (1)
perm (1)
pick (1)
pitch (1)
plan (3)
plant (1)
play (1)
point (1)
polish (1)
pour (1)
pretend (1)
print (1)
protect (1)

pull (1)
push (1)
race (2)
raise (2)
rake (2)
receive (2)
record (1)
recycle (2)
register (1)
relax (1)
remove (2)
rent (1)
repair (1)
repeat (1)
report (1)
request (1)
return (1)
rinse (2)
roast (1)
rock (1)
sauté (2)
save (2)
scrub (3)
seat (1)
sentence (2)
serve (2)
share (2)
shave (2)
ship (3)
shop (3)
shorten (1)
shout (1)
sign (1)
simmer (1)
skate (2)
ski (1)
slice (2)
smell (1)
sneeze (2)
sort (1)
spell (1)
staple (2)

start (1)
stay (1)
steam (1)
stir (3)
stir-fry (4)
stop (3)
stow (1)
stretch (1)
supervise (2)
swallow (1)
tackle (2)
talk (1)
taste (2)
thank (1)
tie (2)
touch (1)
transcribe (2)
transfer (3)
travel (1)
trim (3)
turn (1)
type (2)
underline (2)
unload (1)
unpack (1)
use (2)
vacuum (1)
vomit (1)
vote (2)
wait (1)
walk (1)
wash (1)
watch (1)
water (1)
weed (1)
weigh (1)
wipe (2)
work (1)
wrap (3)
yield (1)

Verb Guide

Irregular Verbs

These verbs have irregular endings in the past and/or the past participle.

The Oxford Picture Dictionary List of Irregular Verbs

simple	past	past participle	simple	past	past participle
be	was	been	leave	left	left
beat	beat	beaten	lend	lent	lent
become	became	become	let	let	let
begin	began	begun	light	lit	lit
bend	bent	bent	make	made	made
bleed	bled	bled	pay	paid	paid
blow	blew	blown	picnic	picnicked	picnicked
break	broke	broken	put	put	put
build	built	built	read	read	read
buy	bought	bought	rewind	rewound	rewound
catch	caught	caught	rewrite	rewrote	rewritten
come	came	come	ride	rode	ridden
cut	cut	cut	run	ran	run
do	did	done	say	said	said
draw	drew	drawn	see	saw	seen
drink	drank	drunk	sell	sold	sold
drive	drove	driven	send	sent	sent
eat	ate	eaten	set	set	set
fall	fell	fallen	sew	sewed	sewn
feed	fed	fed	shoot	shot	shot
feel	felt	felt	sing	sang	sung
find	found	found	sit	sat	sat
fly	flew	flown	speak	spoke	spoken
get	got	gotten	stand	stood	stood
give	gave	given	sweep	swept	swept
go	went	gone	swim	swam	swum
hang	hung	hung	swing	swung	swung
have	had	had	take	took	taken
hear	heard	heard	teach	taught	taught
hide	hid	hidden	throw	threw	thrown
hit	hit	hit	wake	woke	woken
hold	held	held	wear	wore	worn
keep	kept	kept	withdraw	withdrew	withdrawn
lay	laid	laid	write	wrote	written

Index

Two numbers are shown after words in the index: the first refers to the page where the word is illustrated and the second refers to the item number of the word on that page. For example, cool [kōōl] **10**-3 means that the word *cool* is item number 3 on page 10. If only the bold page number appears, then that word is part of the unit title or subtitle, or is found somewhere else on the page. A bold number followed by ◆ means the word can be found in the exercise space at the bottom of that page.

Words or combinations of words that appear in **bold** type are used as verbs or verb phrases. Words used as other parts of speech are shown in ordinary type. So, for example, **file** (in bold type) is the verb *file*, while file (in ordinary type) is the noun *file*. Words or phrases in small capital letters (for example, HOLIDAYS) form unit titles.

Phrases and other words that form combinations with an individual word entry are often listed underneath it. Rather than repeating the word each time it occurs in combination with what is listed under it, the word is replaced by three dots (...), called an ellipsis. For example, under the word *bus*, you will find ...driver and ...stop meaning *bus driver* and *bus stop*. Under the word *store* you will find shoe... and toy..., meaning *shoe store* and *toy store*.

Pronunciation Guide

The index includes a pronunciation guide for all the words and phrases illustrated in the book. This guide uses symbols commonly found in dictionaries for native speakers. These symbols, unlike those used in pronunciation systems such as the International Phonetic Alphabet, tend to use English spelling patterns and so should help you to become more aware of the connections between written English and spoken English.

Consonants

[b] as in back [băk]
[ch] as in cheek [chēk]
[d] as in date [dāt]
[dh] as in this [dhĭs]
[f] as in face [fās]
[g] as in gas [găs]
[h] as in half [hăf]
[j] as in jam [jăm]

[k] as in key [kē]
[l] as in leaf [lēf]
[m] as in match [măch]
[n] as in neck [něk]
[ng] as in ring [rĭng]
[p] as in park [pärk]
[r] as in rice [rīs]
[s] as in sand [sănd]

[sh] as in shoe [shōō]
[t] as in tape [tāp]
[th] as in three [thrē]
[v] as in vine [vīn]
[w] as in wait [wāt]
[y] as in yams [yămz]
[z] as in zoo [zōō]
[zh] as in measure [mězh/ər]

Vowels

[ā] as in bake [bāk]
[ă] as in back [băk]
[ä] as in car [kär] or box [bäks]
[ē] as in beat [bēt]
[ĕ] as in bed [bĕd]
[ë] as in bear [bër]
[ī] as in line [līn]

[ĭ] as in lip [lĭp]
[ï] as in near [nïr]
[ō] as in cold [kōld]
[ö] as in short [shört]
    or claw [klö]
[ōō] as in cool [kōōl]
[ŏŏ] as in cook [kŏŏk]

[ow] as in cow [kow]
[oy] as in boy [boy]
[ŭ] as in cut [kŭt]
[ü] as in curb [kürb]
[ə] as in above [ə bŭv/]

All the pronunciation symbols used are alphabetical except for the schwa [ə]. The schwa is the most frequent vowel sound in English. If you use the schwa appropriately in unstressed syllables, your pronunciation will sound more natural.

Vowels before [r] are shown with the symbol [¨] to call attention to the special quality that vowels have before [r]. (Note that the symbols [ä] and [ö] are also used for vowels not followed by [r], as in *box* or *claw*.) You should listen carefully to native speakers to discover how these vowels actually sound.

Stress

This index follows the system for marking stress used in many dictionaries for native speakers.

1. Stress is not marked if a word consisting of a single syllable occurs by itself.

2. Where stress is marked, two levels are distinguished:

   a bold accent [/] is placed after each syllable with primary (or strong) stress, a light accent [/] is placed after each syllable with secondary (or weaker) stress.

In phrases and other combinations of words, stress is indicated for each word as it would be pronounced within the whole phrase or other unit. If a word consisting of a single syllable is stressed in the combinations listed below it, the accent mark indicating the degree of stress it has in the phrases (primary or secondary) is shown in parentheses. A hyphen replaces any part of a word or phrase that is omitted. For example, bus [bŭs(/–)] shows that the word *bus* is said with primary stress in the combinations shown below it. The word ...driver [–drī/vər], listed under *bus*, shows that *driver* has secondary stress in the combination *bus driver*: [bŭs/ drī/vər].

Syllable Boundaries

Syllable boundaries are indicated by a single space or by a stress mark.

Note: The pronunciations shown in this index are based on patterns of American English. There has been no attempt to represent all of the varieties of American English. Students should listen to native speakers to hear how the language actually sounds in a particular region.

Index

Index

Index

Index

Index

Index

Index

Index

Index

Index

Index

Index

Index

Index

Index

Index

Geographical Index

Continents

Countries and other locations

Geographical Index